Windows® XP
Just the Steps™
FOR
DUMMIES®

by Nancy Stevenson

WILEY

Wiley Publishing, Inc.

Windows® XP Just the Steps™ For Dummies®

Published by
Wiley Publishing, Inc.
111 River Street
Hoboken, NJ 07030-5774

Copyright © 2005 by Wiley Publishing, Inc., Indianapolis, Indiana

Published by Wiley Publishing, Inc., Indianapolis, Indiana

Published simultaneously in Canada

For general information on our other products and services, please contact our Customer Care Department within the U.S. at 800-762-2974, outside the U.S. at 317-572-3993, or fax 317-572-4002.

Wiley also publishes its books in a variety of electronic formats. Some content that appears in print may not be available in electronic books.

Library of Congress Control Number: 2004112342

ISBN: 0-7645-7480-9

Manufactured in the United States of America

10 9 8 7 6 5 4 3 2

1O/QT/RR/QU/IN

WILEY

About the Author

Nancy Stevenson: She is the author of over 40 books on topics ranging from project management to desktop applications and the Internet. She has taught technical writing at the university level, and worked for several years as a manager in both the software and publishing industries. She is currently a freelance writer living in the Pacific Northwest.

Dedication

To my partner in gratitude for his wonderful support and love.

Author's Acknowledgments

Thanks to Wiley for entrusting a book in this new series to me, and to Beth Taylor, intrepid editor, for shepherding the process through and vastly improving my work. Thanks also to Virginia Sanders for her excellent input and to Lee Musick for eagle-eyed technical editing. This one was truly a team effort!

Publisher's Acknowledgments

We're proud of this book; please send us your comments through our online registration form located at `www.dummies.com/register/`. Some of the people who helped bring this book to market include the following:

Acquisitions, Editorial, and Media Development

Project Editor: Beth Taylor

Acquisitions Editor: Tiffany Franklin

Copy Editor: Virginia Sanders

Technical Editor: Lee Musick

Editorial Manager: Leah Cameron

Editorial Assistant: Amanda Foxworth

Cartoons: Rich Tennant, `www.the5thwave.com`

Compostition

Project Coordinator: Nancee Reeves

Layout and Graphics: Andrea Dahl, Lauren Goddard, Denny Hager, Michael Kruzil, Melanee Prendergast, Jacque Roth

Proofreaders: Arielle Carole Mennelle, Dwight Ramsey, Brian H. Walls

Indexer: Lynnzee Elze

Publishing and Editorial for Technology Dummies

Richard Swadley, Vice President and Executive Group Publisher

Andy Cummings, Vice President and Publisher

Mary Bednarek, Executive Acquisitions Director

Mary C. Corder, Editorial Director

Publishing for Consumer Dummies

Diane Graves Steele, Vice President and Publisher

Joyce Pepple, Acquisitions Director

Composition Services

Gerry Fahey, Vice President of Production Services

Debbie Stailey, Director of Composition Services

Contents at a Glance

I'm guessing that you have a healthy dislike of computer books. You don't want to wade through a long tome on Windows XP — you just want to get in, find out how to do something, and get out. You're not alone. I was itching to write a book where I could get right to the details of how to do things and move on. I don't want to bog you down by telling you what I'm going to tell you, saying my piece, and then reviewing what I just said. That's why I was delighted to tackle a *Just the Steps* book on Windows XP.

About This Book

Windows XP is a very robust piece of software with about as much functionality as Einstein on a good day. If you own a Windows XP computer (and I assume you do, or you should rush to the computer store pronto), you spend a lot of time everyday in the Windows XP environment. Knowing how to harness the power of Windows XP is what this book is all about. As the title suggests, I give you just the steps for doing many of the most common Windows XP tasks. This book is all about getting productive right away.

Why You Need This Book

You can't wait weeks to get to know Windows XP. It's where all your software lives and the way you get to your e-mail and documents. You have to understand Windows XP quickly. You might need to poke around Windows and do work while you figure it out. When you hit a bump in the road, you need a quick answer to get you moving again. This book is full of quick, clear steps that keep you moving in high gear.

Introduction

Conventions used in this book

➡ When you have to type something, I put it in **bold** type.

➡ For menu commands, I use the ⇨ symbol to separate menu items. For example, choose Tools⇨Internet Options. The ⇨ symbol is just my way of saying "Choose Internet Options from the Tools menu."

➡ Points of interest in some figures are circled. The text tells you what to look for and the circle makes it easy to find.

 This icon points out insights or helpful suggestions related to the tasks in the step list.

How This Book Is Organized

This book is conveniently divided into several handy parts:

Part I: Working in Windows XP

Here's where you get the basics of opening and closing software applications, working with files and folders to manage the documents you create, and using built-in Windows applications, such as the calculator and WordPad.

Part II: Getting on the Internet

The whole world is online, and you don't want to be left out. Here's where I show you how to connect, how to browse, and how to use e-mail.

Part III: Setting Up Hardware and Maintaining Your System

Windows can use a little help sometimes. You might have to make a little effort to set up new hardware or clean up the Windows system. This part is where I show you how to do that.

Part IV: Customizing Windows

You probably want Windows to function in a way that matches your style. This is the part where I cover customizing the look of Windows, customizing it's behavior, and keeping it secure.

Part V: Fixing Common Problems

Yes, I admit it, even Windows can have problems. Luckily, it also has tools to get you out of trouble. In this part, I explain how to deal with hardware and software problems, as well as how to get help when you need it.

Part VI: Fun and Games with Windows

Go to these chapters to discover a fun world of games, music, and video just waiting for you in Windows XP.

Part VII: Practical Applications

Go to these chapters to discover how to work remotely and use Windows-based applications. You also find projects to try using Windows XP.

Get Ready To

Whether you need to open a piece of software and get working, check your e-mail, or get online, just browse this book, pick a task, and jump in. Windows XP can be your best friend if you know how to use it, and the tasks that I cover in this book can make you a Windows XP master in no time.

Part I
Working in Windows XP

The 5th Wave   By Rich Tennant

"I'm ordering our new PC. Do you want
it left-brain- or right-brain-oriented?"

Controlling Applications under Windows

Chapter 1

You might think of Windows XP as a set of cool accessories, such as games, a calculator, and an address book, but Windows is first and foremost an operating system. Windows' main purpose is to enable you to run and manage other software applications, from word processing and spreadsheet programs to the latest 3D computer action game. Using the best methods for accessing and running software with Windows saves you time, and setting up Windows XP in the way that works best for you can make your life easier.

In this chapter, you explore several simple and very handy techniques for launching and moving among applications. You go through step-by-step procedures ranging from installing software to removing it, and from logging on to Windows to shutting down your computer. Along the way, you discover the Windows Start Menu (a command central for running programs) and the Quick Launch bar (which might sound like a salad bar at a fast food restaurant, but it's actually the area of the Windows taskbar that lets you open frequently used programs).

Here, then, are the procedures that you can use to launch, navigate, and organize programs in Windows XP.

Get ready to . . .

Log On to Windows

1. Turn on your computer to begin the Windows start up sequence. (*Note:* If you haven't set up the password protection feature, you're taken directly to the Windows desktop, as shown in Figure 1-1.)

2. In the resulting Windows Welcome screen, enter a password and click the green arrow button. Windows verifies your password and displays the Windows desktop.

To log on as another user (for example, if somebody else in your family is logged on and you want to change to your user account), choose Start➪Log Off. Click the Switch User button. Click your user name in the list of users that appears (the same list that you see on the Windows Welcome screen), and then follow the steps in this task to finish logging on.

Install Software

1. If you insert a software CD and nothing happens, choose Start➪Control Panel and click the Add or Remove Programs icon to open the Add or Remove Programs window.

In many cases, you don't need to go through Windows to install software. Just pop the software CD into your CD drive, and the installation process begins. Give Windows a vacation — after all, it works hard day after day, right?

2. Click the Add New Programs button on the left and then click the CD or Floppy button, shown in Figure 1-2.

Figure 1-1: The Windows desktop

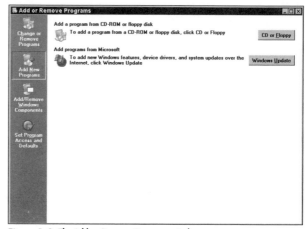

Figure 1-2: The Add or Remove Programs window

3. When the resulting Install Program from CD or Floppy dialog box appears (see Figure 1-3), click Next to run the software.

4. Follow the prompts for that software installation. (*Note:* Some programs require that you reboot your computer, so turn it off and then on to complete the setup of the new program.)

 If you install software and later want to change which features of the program have been installed, go to the Control Panel. When you choose Add or Remove Programs, find the software in the list that appears and click the Change/Remove button.

Open an Application

1. Open an application by using any of the following three methods:

   • Choose Start⇨All Programs. Locate the program name on the All Programs menu and click it; if clicking it displays a submenu, click the program item on that menu (as shown in Figure 1-4).

   • Double-click a program shortcut icon on the desktop.

   • Press the Windows key to display the taskbar if it's hidden and then click an icon on the Quick Launch bar, just to the right of the Start button.

2. When the application opens, if it's a game, play it; if it's a spreadsheet, enter numbers into it; if it's your e-mail program, start deleting junk mail . . . you get the idea.

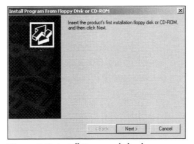

Figure 1-3: Install Program dialog box

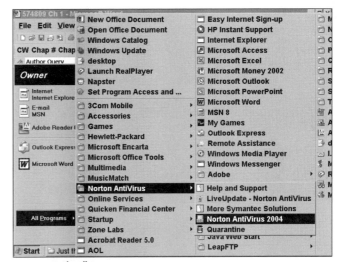

Figure 1-4: The All Programs menu

 Not every program that's installed on your computer appears as a desktop shortcut or Quick Launch bar icon. To add a program to the Quick Launch bar, see the task "Utilize the Quick Launch Bar," later in this chapter. To add a desktop shortcut, see Chapter 2.

Resize an Application Window

1. With an application open and maximized, click the Restore Down button (looks like two overlapping windows) in the top-right corner of the program window.

2. To enlarge a minimized application to fill the screen, click the Maximize button (see Figure 1-5). (*Note:* This is in the same place as the Restore Down button, and the button that appears depends on whether you have the screen reduced in size or maximized. A ScreenTip identifies the button when you pass your mouse over it.)

 With a window maximized, you can't move the window around on the desktop, which is one way to view more than one window on your screen at the same time. If you reduce a window in size, you can then click and hold the title bar to drag the window around on the desktop. You can also click and drag the corners of the window to resize it any way you want.

Switch between Running Applications

1. Open two or more programs. The last program that you open is the active program.

2. Press and hold Alt+Tab to open a small box, shown in Figure 1-6, revealing all opened programs.

3. Release the Tab key, but keep Alt held down. Press Tab to cycle through the icons representing open programs.

4. Release the Alt key, and Windows switches to whichever program is selected. To switch back to the last program that was active, simply press Alt+Tab, and that program becomes the active program once again.

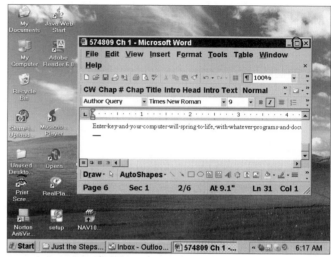

Figure 1-5: Maximize the minimized Microsoft Word file

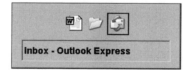

Figure 1-6: Open programs in Windows

 All open programs also appear as items on the Windows taskbar. You can click any running program on the taskbar to make it the active program. If the taskbar isn't visible, press the Windows key to display it.

Move Information between Applications

1. Open two applications and, if their windows are maximized, click the Restore Down buttons in the upper-right corners to reduce their sizes.

2. Click the bottom-right corner of each program window and drag to change the size further until you can see both programs on the Windows desktop at once (see Figure 1-7).

3. Click and hold their title bars to drag the windows around on your desktop or right-click the taskbar and choose Tile Horizontally or Tile Vertically to arrange the windows on the desktop.

4. Select the information that you want to move (for example text, numbers, or a graphical object). Right-click the selection and drag it to the other application document.

5. Release your mouse, and the shortcut menu shown in Figure 1-8 appears. Choose Move Here to move it, or choose Copy Here to place a copy in the new location.

 You can also use simple cut-and-paste or copy-and-paste operations to take information from one application and move it or place a copy of it into a document in another application. In addition, some applications have Export or Send To commands to send the contents of a document to another application. For example, Microsoft Word has a Send To➪Microsoft Office PowerPoint command to quickly send a Word document to be the basis of a PowerPoint presentation outline.

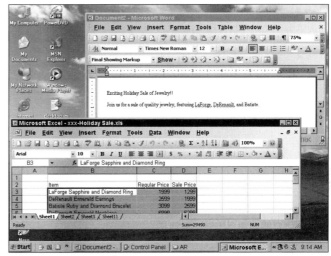

Figure 1-7: Arranging windows

Figure 1-8: Shortcut menu

Utilize the Quick Launch Bar

1. Locate the Quick Launch bar on the taskbar just to the right of the Start button; if it's not visible, right-click the taskbar and choose Toolbars➪Quick Launch from the shortcut menu (see Figure 1-9). By default, it includes the Show Desktop icon and some Microsoft programs, such as Internet Explorer and Outlook.

 The Quick Launch bar is a feature of the taskbar. If it doesn't appear, from the Windows desktop, right-click the taskbar and choose Toolbars ➪Quick Launch.

2. To place any application on the Quick Launch bar, shown in Figure 1-10, click that application's icon (or *shortcut*) on the Windows desktop and drag it to the Quick Launch bar. (If you want help creating a desktop shortcut, see Chapter 2.)

 If you have more programs in this area than can be shown on the taskbar, click the arrows to the right of the Quick Launch bar and a shortcut menu of programs appears. However, don't clutter up your Quick Launch bar, which can make it unwieldy. Logical candidates to place here are your Internet browser, your e-mail program, and programs that you use every day, such as a word processor or a calendar program.

 When the Quick Launch bar is displayed, the Show Desktop button is available. When you click this button, all open applications are reduced to taskbar icons. It's a quick way to clean your desktop or hide what you're up to!

Figure 1-9: The Toolbars menu

Figure 1-10: Icons on the Quick Launch bar

Organize the Start Menu

1. Press the Windows key to display the Start menu. Right-click anywhere on an empty part of the Start menu and choose Properties.

2. In the resulting Taskbar and Start Menu Properties dialog box, click the Customize button to display the Customize Start Menu dialog box shown in Figure 1-11. You can do the following:

   - Click the up or down arrows on the Number of Programs on Start Menu text box to display more or fewer of your frequently used programs.

   - Use the drop-down lists of alternate Internet and E-Mail programs to select different applications to appear on the Start menu.

3. Click the Advanced tab to display it. Determine what items you want to display on the Start menu and select or deselect items in the Start Menu Items list.

4. After you finish making selections, click OK to save the new settings. Your Start menu now reflects your changes, showing items for accessing and running programs and features, such as the ones in Figure 1-12.

 Right-click the list of programs and choose Sort By Name to alphabetize the list. Folders get reordered to appear first, and then individual programs.

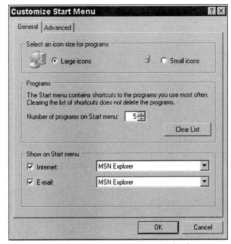

Figure 1-11: The Customize Start Menu dialog box

Figure 1-12: A typical Start menu, customized for the programs I use most

Start an Application Automatically

1. Right-click the Start menu button and choose Explore, as shown in Figure 1-13.

2. In the resulting Windows Explorer dialog box is a list of folders on the left side. Click the plus sign next to the Start Menu folder, then the Programs folder, and then the Startup folder to see a list of programs in it.

3. Click a program from the list and drag it into the Startup folder (see Figure 1-14).

4. When you finish moving programs into the Startup folder, click the Close button in the upper-right corner.

 In this procedure, you change to the Classic Start menu style. This gives your Start menu a different appearance, used in earlier versions of Windows. Here items are organized differently and fewer options are offered. To display the Taskbar and Start Menu dialog box with this style displayed, you must choose Settings⇨Taskbar and Start Menu.

 You can remove an application from the Start menu by right-clicking the Start button and choosing Properties. On the Start Menu tab, click the Customize button. In the Customize dialog box, click the Advanced tab and then clear the check box for the item you want to remove.

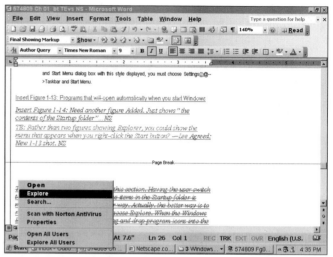

Figure 1-13: Opening Windows Explorer

Figure 1-14: The Startup folder contents

Set Program Access Defaults

1. Choose Start⇨All Programs⇨Set Program Access and Defaults.

2. In the resulting Add or Remove Programs window, shown in Figure 1-15, click the arrow next to any of the choices to see specifics about the programs that they set as defaults.

3. Select one of the following options to see detailed information (shown in Figure 1-16):

   - **Computer Manufacturer:** Restores defaults set when your computer shipped. Your version of Windows XP may or may not have been set up with this option by your computer manufacturer.

   - **Microsoft Windows:** Sets defaults used by Windows.

   - **Non-Microsoft:** Removes access to Microsoft programs and uses currently set-up programs as defaults. This is popular with Linux users and Microsoft haters.

   - **Custom:** Allows you to set up the programs that you have currently set as default, Microsoft programs, or a combination.

4. Click OK when you've made your settings to save them.

 When you deselect the Enable Access to this Program option in the Custom option, you don't find it on the Start menu any longer. It's still on your hard drive, though, and you can open it by using Windows Explorer.

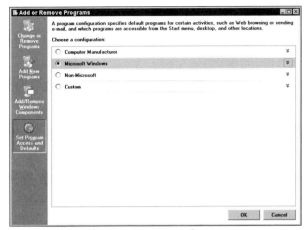

Figure 1-15: The Add or Remove Programs window

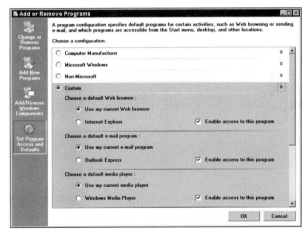

Figure 1-16: Various custom access options

Remove an Application

1. Choose Start⇨Control Panel⇨Add or Remove Programs.

2. In the resulting Add or Remove Programs window, shown in Figure 1-17, click a program and then click the Remove button.

3. If you're sure that you want to remove the program, click Yes in the confirmation dialog box shown in Figure 1-18. A dialog box shows the progress of the procedure; it disappears when the program has been removed.

4. Click the Close button to close the Add or Remove Programs dialog box.

 With some programs that include multiple applications, such as Microsoft Office, you might want to remove only one program, not the whole shooting match. For example, you might decide that you have no earthly use for Access, but can't let a day go by without using Excel and Word, so why not free up some hard drive space and send Access packing? If you want to modify a program in this way, click the Change button in Step 2, rather than the Remove button. The dialog box that appears allows you to select the programs that you want to install or uninstall.

 Warning: If you click the Change or Remove Programs link, there are some programs that will simply be removed with no further input from you. Be really sure that you don't need a program before you remove it.

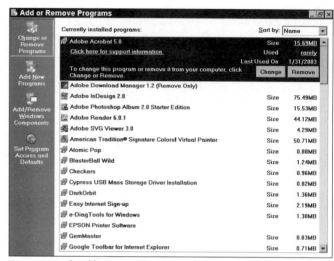

Figure 1-17: The Add or Remove Programs window

Figure 1-18: The confirmation dialog box

Run Windows Update

1. Connect to the Internet, and then choose Start⇨All Programs⇨Windows Update.

2. On the resulting Windows Update Web page, click the Scan for Updates link, shown in Figure 1-19.

3. When the scan is complete, the Pick Updates to Install page appears. Click the Review and Install Updates link.

4. On the resulting Web page, use the scrollbar to review the recommended updates, clicking the Remove button for any that you don't want to install.

5. Click Install Now to see the progress of the downloads (see Figure 1-20).

 Updates typically include security updates to Microsoft products, updated drivers for peripherals such as printers, mouse, and monitors, and updates to Microsoft products to fix *bugs,* as they're affectionately known among computer geeks. Bugs are bad, but updates are usually good.

 Warning: If you're running Windows XP on a network, it's possible that your network security settings could stop you from using the Windows Update feature. However, the good news is that if you're on a network, your network administrator should be taking care of all that stuff for you.

Figure 1-19: The opening window of Windows Update

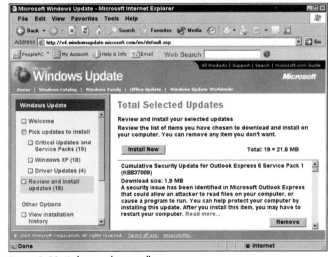

Figure 1-20: Updates ready to install

Shut Down Your Computer

1. Choose Start⇨Turn Off Computer.

2. In the resulting Turn Off Computer dialog box shown in Figure 1-21, click the Turn Off button to shut down the computer completely; if you want to *reboot* (turn off and turn on) your computer, click the Restart button.

If you're going away for a while but don't want to have to go through the whole booting up sequence complete with Windows music when you return, you don't have to turn off your computer. Just click the Stand By button in Step 2 to put your computer into a kind of sleeping state where the screen goes black and the fan shuts down. When you get back, click your mouse button or press Enter and your computer springs to life, and whatever programs and documents you had open are still intact.

Figure 1-21: The Turn Off Computer dialog box

Working with Files and Folders

*J*oin me for a moment in the office of yesterday. Notice all the metal filing cabinets and Manila file folders holding paper rather than sleek computer workstations and wireless Internet connections.

Fast forward to today: You still organize the work you do every day in files and folders, but today, the metal and cardboard have been dropped in favor of electronic bits and bytes. Files are the individual documents that you save from within applications such as Word and Excel, and you use folders and subfolders to organize several files into groups or categories, such as by project or by customer.

In this chapter, you find out how to organize and work with files and folders, including:

- **Finding your way around files and folders:** This includes tasks such as locating and opening files and folders.

- **Manipulating files and folders:** These tasks cover moving, renaming, deleting, and printing a file.

- **Squeezing a file's contents.** This is where you hear all about creating a compressed folder to reduce a large file to a more manageable creature.

Chapter 2

Get ready to . . .

Launch a Recently Used Document

1. Open the Start menu and right-click any blank area or the title bar.

2. In the resulting shortcut menu, choose Properties.

3. In the Properties dialog box, click the Start Menu tab (if that tab isn't already displayed) and then click the Customize button.

4. In the Customize Start Menu dialog box, display the Advanced tab (see Figure 2-1).

5. Make sure that the List My Most Recently Opened Documents check box is selected and then click OK twice.

6. Choose Start⇨My Recent Documents and then click a file in the resulting submenu (see Figure 2-2) to open it.

 If a file in the My Recent Document list can be opened with more than one application — for example, a graphics file that you might open with Paint or Windows Picture and Fax Viewer — you can right-click the file and use the Open With command to control which application you use to open the file.

Figure 2-1: The Advanced tab in the Customize Start Menu dialog box

Figure 2-2: The My Recent Documents item that now appears on the Start menu

Locate Files and Folders in My Computer

1. Choose Start⇨My Computer.

2. In the My Computer window (see Figure 2-3), double-click an item, such as a floppy drive, CD-ROM drive, or your computer hard drive to open it.

3. In the resulting window (see Figure 2-4 for an example), if the file that you want is stored within a folder, double-click the folder or a series of folders until you locate it.

4. When you find the file you want, double-click it to open it.

 Note: File and Folder Tasks area is on the left side of the window in Figure 2-4. Use the commands in this area to perform common file and folder tasks, such as e-mailing a file or folder, copying it, deleting it, or moving it.

 Note: Depending on how you've chosen to display files and folders, you may see text listings as in Figure 2-4, icons, or even thumbnail representations of file contents.

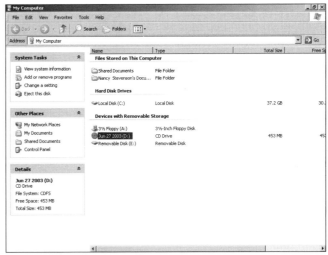

Figure 2-3: The My Computer window

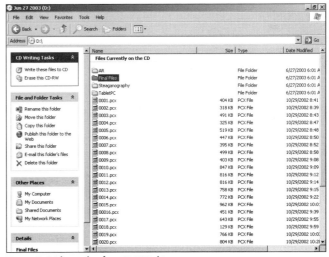

Figure 2-4: The window for a CD-ROM drive

Locate Files and Folders in Windows Explorer

1. Choose Start⇨All Programs⇨Accessories⇨Windows Explorer.

2. In the Windows Explorer window, shown in Figure 2-5, double-click the folder or click the plus sign to the left of a folder in the Folders pane along the left side to obtain the file inside the folder.

3. The folder's contents are shown on the right in Explorer. If necessary, open a series of folders in this manner until you locate the file you want.

4. When you find the file you want, double-click it to open it.

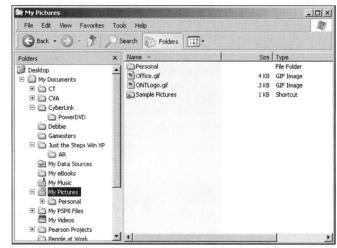

Figure 2-5: The Windows Explorer window

 To see different perspectives and information about files in Windows Explorer, click the arrow on the View button (it looks like a little window with blue title bar across the top) and choose one of the following menu options: Thumbnails for graphical representations of file contents; Tiles or Icons to see folder and file icons in different arrangements; List for a list of file and folder names with small icon symbols; or Details to add details such as file type and size to the file list.

 If you are still having trouble finding the folder or file you want, consider changing the view by clicking the View button in the My Documents window to show information such as file size and date last modified. This may help you identify the specific file you want.

Search for a File

1. Choose Start➪Search.

2. In the resulting Search Results window, click the arrow for the type of item for which you want to search (for example Pictures, Music, or Video or Documents).

3. In the resulting window (see Figure 2-6), select any of the criteria and then enter a word or phrase to search by. Click Search.

4. Click the Sort Results by Category or View Results Differently arrows to get a different perspective on your results:

    *   Sort Results by Category (see Figure 2-7) allows you to sort results by name, date last modified, size, or file type.

    *   View Results Differently lets you select different graphical or text representations of results, such as thumbnails or details.

5. Click any of the arrows under No, Refine This Search to search again.

6. When you locate the file you wanted, you can double-click it to open it.

 When you're in the Search Results window in Step 2 where you choose the type of file to search for, notice the Use Advanced Search Options button. If you click this button, additional options appear, including a keyword feature for words or phrases contained within documents, a field to specify the search location, and a way to specify file size.

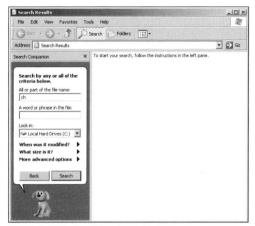

Figure 2-6: The Search Results window

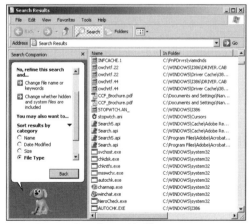

Figure 2-7: Search results sorted by file type

Move a File or Folder

1. Choose Start➪All Programs➪Accessories➪Windows Explorer.

2. In the Windows Explorer window (see Figure 2-8) double-click a folder or series of folders to locate the file that you want to move.

3. Do one of the following actions:

   • Click and drag the file to another folder in the Folders pane on the left side of the window. If you use right-click and drag, you are offered the options of moving or copying the item when you place it via a smart-tag (a little icon that appears).

   • Right-click the file and choose Send To. Then choose from the options shown in the submenu that appears (shown in Figure 2-9).

4. Click the Close button in the upper-right corner of the Windows Explorer window to close it.

 To view files on your storage media (such as a CD-ROM drive), scroll to the bottom of the Folders pane in Windows Explorer and click My Computer. You see your hard drive and any removable storage media displayed in the right-side pane. Double-click any item to display the files and folders contained there.

Rename a File or Folder

1. Locate the file that you want to rename by using Windows Explorer. (Choose Start➪All Programs➪ Accessories➪Windows Explorer.)

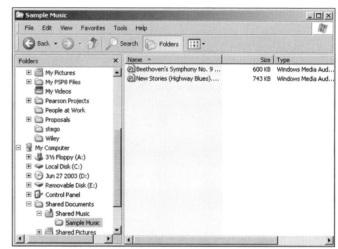

Figure 2-8: The Windows Explorer window

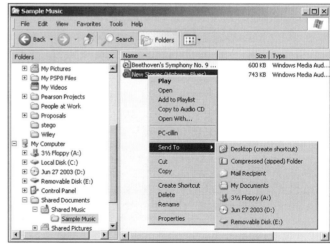

Figure 2-9: The Send To submenu

2. Right-click the file and choose Rename (see Figure 2-10).

3. The filename is now available for editing. Type a new name, and then click anywhere outside the filename to save the new name.

 You can't rename a file to have the same name as another file located in the same folder. To give a file the same name as another, cut it from its current location, paste it into another folder, and then follow the procedure in this task. Or, open the file and save it to a new location with the same name, which creates a copy.

Print a File

1. Open the file in the application that it was created in.

2. Choose File⇨Print.

3. In the resulting Print dialog box (see Figure 2-11) select what to print; these options might vary, but generally include:

   • **All:** Prints all pages in the document.

   • **Current page:** Prints whatever page your cursor is active in at the moment.

   • **Pages:** Prints a page range or series of pages you enter in that field. For example, enter **3-11** to print pages 3 through 11, or enter **3, 7, 9-11** to print pages 3, 7, and 9 through 11.

   • **Selection:** Prints any text or objects that you have selected when you choose the Print command.

4. In the Copies field, click the up or down arrow to set the number of copies to make; if you want multiple copies collated, select the Collate check box.

5. Click OK to proceed with printing.

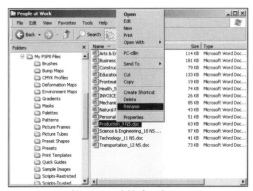

Figure 2-10: A filename available for editing

 Here's another method for printing: locate the file by using Windows Explorer (choose Start⇨All Programs⇨Accessories⇨Windows Explorer). Right-click the file and choose Print from the shortcut menu that appears. The file prints with your default printer settings.

 Different applications might offer different options in the Print dialog box. For example, PowerPoint offers several options for what to print, including slides, handouts, or the presentation outline, and Outlook allows you to print e-mails in table or memo styles.

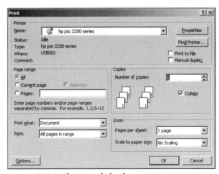

Figure 2-11: The Print dialog box

Create a Shortcut to a File or Folder

1. Locate the file or folder by using Windows Explorer. (Choose Start➪All Programs➪Accessories➪Windows Explorer.)

2. In the resulting Windows Explorer window (see Figure 2-12), right-click the file or folder that you want to create a shortcut for and choose Create Shortcut.

3. A shortcut named Shortcut to File or Folder Name appears at the bottom of the currently open folder. Click the shortcut and drag it to the desktop.

 To open the file in its originating application or a folder in Windows Explorer, simply double-click the desktop shortcut icon.

Delete a File or Folder

1. Locate the file or folder by using Windows Explorer. (Choose Start➪All Programs➪Accessories➪Windows Explorer.)

2. In the resulting Windows Explorer window, right-click the file or folder that you want to delete and choose Delete.

3. In the resulting dialog box (see Figure 2-13), click Yes to delete the file.

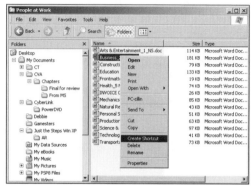

Figure 2-12: The Windows Explorer window displaying a shortcut menu

 When you delete a file or folder in Windows, it's not really gone. It's removed to the Recycle Bin. Windows periodically purges older files from this folder, but you might still be able to retrieve recently deleted files and folders from it. To try to restore a deleted file or folder, double-click the Recycle Bin icon on the desktop. Right-click the file or folder and choose Restore. Windows restores the file to where it was when you deleted it.

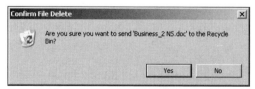

Figure 2-13: The Confirm File Delete dialog box

Create a Compressed Folder

1. Locate the files or folders that you want to compress by using Windows Explorer. (Choose Start➪All Programs➪ Accessories➪Windows Explorer.)

2. In the resulting Windows Explorer window, you can do the following (shown in Figure 2-14):

   - **Select a series of files or folders:** Click a file or folder, press and hold Shift to select a series of items listed consecutively in the folder, and click the final item.

   - **Select non-consecutive items:** Press Ctrl and click the items.

3. Right-click your selected items; in the resulting shortcut menu (see Figure 2-15), choose Send To➪Compressed (Zipped) Folder. A new compressed folder appears. The folder icon is named after the last file you selected in the series.

 You might want to rename a compressed folder with a name other than the one that Windows automatically assigns to it. See the task "Rename a File or Folder" in this chapter to find out just how to do that.

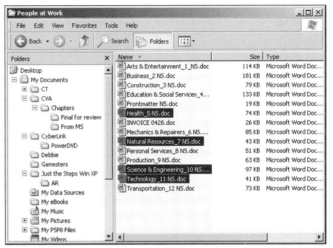

Figure 2-14: A series of selected files and folders

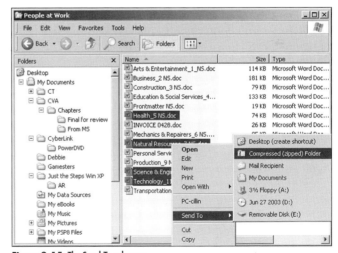

Figure 2-15: The Send To submenu

Add a File to Your Favorites List

1. Open Windows Explorer. (Choose Start⇨All Programs⇨ Accessories⇨Windows Explorer.)

2. In the resulting Windows Explorer window, click a file or folder and choose Favorites⇨Add to Favorites.

3. In the dialog box that appears, enter a name to be displayed in the Favorites list for the file or folder, and then click OK (see Figure 2-16).

4. To see a list of your Favorites, choose Start⇨Favorites.

5. In the resulting submenu (see Figure 2-17), click an item to open it.

 If the Favorites item doesn't display on your Start menu, right-click the Start menu and choose Properties. On the Start Menu tab with Start Menu selected, click the Customize button. Click the Advanced tab to display it, make sure that Favorites is selected, and then click OK twice to save the setting.

Figure 2-16: The Favorites menu in Windows Explorer

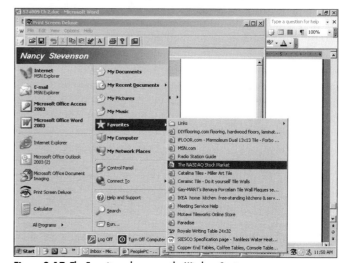

Figure 2-17: The Favorites submenu on the Windows Start menu

Using Built-In Windows Applications

Chapter 3

Windows XP isn't just a traffic cop for your computer's hardware and other software programs; it has its own set of neat tools that you can use to get things done. Using various Windows accessories (that is, built-in software programs), you can do everything from writing down great thoughts to working with beautiful pictures. Here's what Windows' built-in applications help you do:

➡ **Work with words:** WordPad is your best bet for documents with graphics and formatting, and NotePad is an ideal place for plain text or to write the code behind Web pages.

➡ **Manipulate numbers:** The Windows Calculator doesn't fit in the palm of your hand, but it does offer a little on-screen calculator that you can use to push numbers around.

➡ **Play with images:** Windows makes you an artist by letting you view and edit graphics files in Paint, view digital images (you know, the photos you took at little Ricky's birthday party) in Windows Picture and Fax Viewer, and make your scanner easy to work with the Scanner and Camera Wizard.

➡ **Manage contacts and communicate:** Windows Address Book is an electronic version of that little alphabetical book you keep by your phone; it's a great place to store contact information. Windows Messenger is an instant messaging program that allows you to chat online in real time with anybody who's online.

Get ready to . . .

Create a Formatted Document in WordPad

1. Choose Start➪All Programs➪Accessories➪WordPad to open the WordPad window.

2. Enter text in the blank document. (*Note:* Press Enter to create blank lines between text.)

3. Click and drag to select the text, and then choose Format➪Font.

4. In the resulting Font dialog box, shown in Figure 3-1, adjust the settings for Font, Font Style, or Font Size (see Figure 3-2) and apply strikeout or underline effects by selecting those check boxes. You can also modify the font color. Click OK to apply the settings.

5. Click various other tools, such as the alignment buttons or the bullet style button on the toolbar to format selected text.

6. Choose Insert➪Object to insert an object.

7. In the Object dialog box that appears, click the Create New option, click an object type, and then click OK. Modify the inserted object however you want (moving it, resizing it, and so on).

8. When your document is complete, choose File➪Save. In the Save As dialog box, enter a name in the File Name text box, select a file location from the Save In drop-down list, and then click Save.

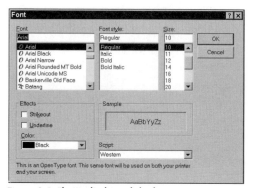

Figure 3-1: The WordPad Font dialog box

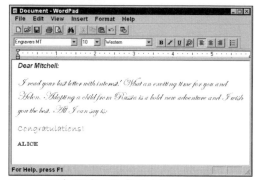

Figure 3-2: The Windows WordPad window

 To e-mail a copy of your WordPad document is simplicity itself. Just choose File➪Send, and an e-mail form appears from your default e-mail program with the file already attached. Just enter a recipient and a message and click Send. It's on its way!

Create a Text File in NotePad

1. Choose Start➪All Programs➪Accessories➪NotePad. The NotePad window appears with a blank document open.

2. In the resulting NotePad window (shown in Figure 3-3), enter text for your document. When you reach the right margin, the text should wrap to the next line automatically. (If wrapping isn't automatic, choose Format➪Word Wrap to make it so.) To place blank lines between text, press Enter. (*Note:* Use the Edit menu commands, Cut, Copy, and Paste, to edit what you write.)

3. Click and drag over the text to select it, and then choose Format➪Font.

4. In the resulting Font dialog box, shown in Figure 3-4, use the Font, Font Style, and Size text lists to make formatting choices. The Sample area displays the new formatting as you make your choices.

5. After you adjust all your formatting settings, click OK to apply them to the selected text.

 NotePad is a down-and-dirty word processor, meaning that it has few bells and whistles. It has no spell checker, paragraph formatting, tabs, or drawing tools. It's often used by programmers and Web designers as a simple text editor for code that doesn't have to look pretty — it just needs to get the job done. On the other hand, NotePad does have a Find feature, simplified Page Setup and Print features, and my very favorite word processing feature, Undo. So when the job is simple and no other program is available, consider using NotePad.

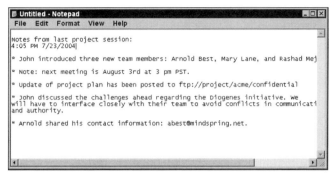

Figure 3-3: The Windows NotePad window

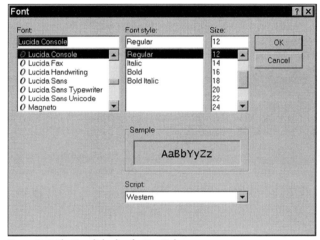

Figure 3-4: The Font dialog box for NotePad

Use the Windows Calculator

1. Choose Start➪All Programs➪Accessories➪Calculator.

2. In the resulting Calculator window (shown in Figure 3-5), you can enter numbers and symbols in a few different ways:

   • Type numbers and symbols on your keyboard and they appear in the entry box of the calculator. Press Enter to perform the calculation.

   • Click numbers or symbols on the calculator display and click the = button to perform the calculation.

3. When you don't need the calculator anymore, you have two options:

   • Click the Minimize button to shrink the window; it now appears as an icon in the taskbar that you can simply click to maximize the window again if you need the calculator later.

   • Click the Close button to close the window. To open it again, you have to go through the Start menu.

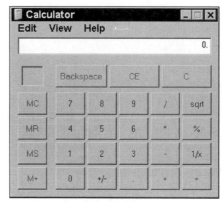

Figure 3-5: The Calculator window

 You can enter calculations by using only keyboard entries. For example, to divide 22 by 2, type **22/2**, and then press Enter. Use the plus, minus, and asterisk (multiply) symbols in this same way.

 If you're the scientific type, try displaying the scientific calculator by choosing View➪Scientific. Now you can play with things that are Greek to me, like cosines, logarithms, and pi. (Okay, I know what pi is; it goes on forever, just like Madonna.) With the Scientific view displayed, additional choices become available on the View menu, such as changing from decimal to binary or degrees to radians. Math geeks, rejoice!

Edit a Picture in Paint

1. Choose Start⇨All Programs⇨Accessories⇨Paint.

2. In the resulting Paint window, choose File⇨Open. Locate a picture file that you want to edit (see Figure 3-6), select it, and click Open. A pretty picture of my house is shown in the Paint window in Figure 3-7.

3. Now you can edit the picture in any number of ways:

   • **Edit colors:** Choose a color from the color palette in the bottom-left corner and use various tools (such as Airbrush, Brush, Fill with Color, and the Color dropper) to apply color to the image or selected drawn objects, such as rectangles.

   • **Select areas:** Select the Free Form Select and Select tools and then click and drag on the image to select portions of the picture. You can then crop out these elements by choosing Edit⇨Cut.

   • **Add text:** Select the Text tool and then click and drag on the image to create a text box in which you can enter and format text.

   • **Draw objects:** Select the Rectangle, Rounded Rectangle, Polygon, or Ellipse tool, and then click and drag on the image to draw objects.

   • **Modify the image:** Use the commands on the Image menu to change the colors and stretch out, flip around, or change the size of the image.

4. Choose File⇨Save to save your masterpiece, File⇨Print to print it, or choose File⇨Send to send it by e-mail.

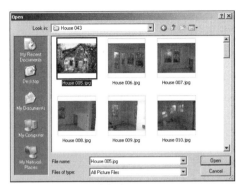

Figure 3-6: The Open dialog box

Figure 3-7: A picture opened in Paint

View a Digital Image in Windows Picture and Fax Viewer

1. Locate an image file on your hard drive, network, or storage media by using Windows Explorer. (Choose Start⇨All Programs⇨Accessories⇨Windows Explorer.)

2. Right-click the filename or icon and choose Open With⇨Windows Picture and Fax Viewer. In the resulting Windows Picture and Fax Viewer, shown in Figure 3-8, you can use the tools at the bottom to do any of the following:

   - The Next Image and Previous Image icons move to a previous or following image in the same folder.

   - The Best Fit and Actual Size icons modify the display of the image in the Picture and Fax Viewer.

   - The Start Slide Show icon begins a full-screen slide show of images.

   - The Zoom In and Zoom Out icons enlarge or shrink the image display.

   - The Rotate Clockwise and Rotate Counterclockwise icons spin the image 90 degrees at a time (see Figure 3-9).

   - Delete, Print, Copy To, and Close All do what their names say.

3. When you finish viewing images, click the Close button in the top-right corner to close the Viewer.

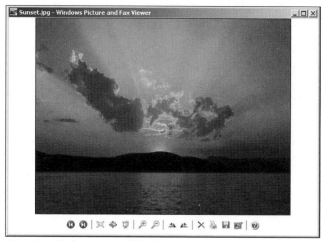

Figure 3-8: Windows Picture and Fax Viewer

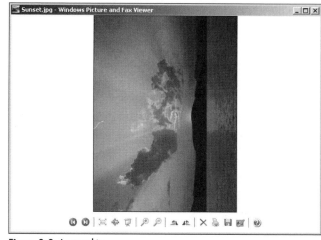

Figure 3-9: A rotated image

Use the Scanner and Camera Wizard

1. Place a page, a picture, or some other object (like those cereal box tops you've been collecting) in your scanner.

2. Choose Start⇨All Programs⇨Accessories⇨Scanner and Camera Wizard. Windows begins scanning your item.

3. On the second wizard screen that appears, you choose your preferences for scanning by clicking one of these radio buttons: Color Picture, Grayscale Picture, Black and White Picture or Text, or Custom. Click Next.

4. In the resulting Scanner and Camera Wizard, you designate information about the file and then click Next:

   • In the first drop-down list (labeled 1 in Figure 3-10), enter a name for a group of pictures or select a group that you've already created.

   • In the second drop-down list (labeled 2), select a format for the file, such as .bmp or .jpg.

   • In the third drop-down list (labeled 3), enter a location to store the file.

5. On the resulting screen, you see that the image is being scanned. Sit tight or go grab a soda while your scanner and computer do their thing.

6. When the scanning is complete, you have three options (see Figure 3-11); choose one, and follow any one of these options to complete working with your pictures:

   • Publish these pictures to a Web site.

   • Order prints of these pictures from a photo printing Web site.

   • Nothing. I'm finished working with these pictures.

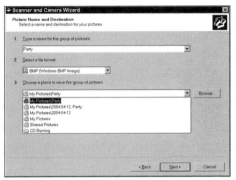

Figure 3-10: The Scanner and Camera Wizard

 If you have more than one device, you get a Select Device dialog box where you choose which one you want to use. Select one and then click OK. Then you see the opening window of the Scanner and Camera Wizard where you have to click Next. You now see the dialog box that I describe in Step 3.

 If you choose Nothing, you get the final wizard window confirming you scanned one item and click Finish. After clicking Finish, you are taken to Windows Explorer, where the file you scanned is highlighted and ready to double-click and edit or view.

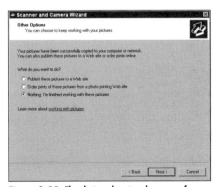

Figure 3-11: The choices the wizard presents for working with a scanned image

Enter Contacts in Windows Address Book

1. Choose Start⇨All Programs⇨Accessories⇨Address Book. You might get a dialog box asking whether you want to make this your default vCard viewer. Click Yes or No depending on your preference.

2. In the Address Book window shown in Figure 3-12, click the New button, and select New Contact from the drop-down list that appears.

3. In the Properties dialog box shown in Figure 3-13, enter information in various fields, clicking on other various tabs to add more details. For some fields, such as E-Mail Addresses, you must enter information and then click the Add button to add it to a list.

4. When you finish entering information, click OK.

 If the contact has more than one e-mail address, select the one you want to most often send e-mail to and click the Set as Default button. This is the address any e-mails will be addressed to.

 To quickly search your Address Book, choose Start⇨Search, click the Other Search Options link, and then click the Computers or People link in the Search window. To start your search, click the link labeled People in Your Address Book. You can then define criteria, such as address, phone number, or e-mail address to search by.

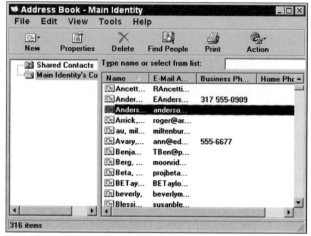

Figure 3-12: Windows Address Book

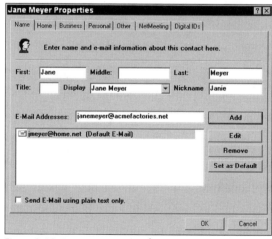

Figure 3-13: Entering new contact information

Add a Contact to Windows Messenger

1. Choose Start⇨All Programs⇨Windows Messenger.

2. In the Windows Messenger window, click the Click Here to Sign In link. If you don't have a .NET Passport, you will be prompted to sign up for one. Enter required information in the series of screens that appears. (If you already have a passport, you're signed in automatically and can skip this step).

3. Click the Add a Contact link in the Windows Messenger window shown in Figure 3-14.

4. In the Add a Contact dialog box that appears, click Next to accept the default option of entering your contact's information.

5. In the next Add a Contact dialog box, enter the person's e-mail address and click Next. The person must have a .NET passport to be accepted as a Windows Messenger contact.

6. In the Windows Messenger dialog box that appears, click one of the two radio buttons and then click OK:

   • Allow this person to see when you are online and contact you.

   • Block this person from seeing when you are online and contacting you

7. To send an e-mail notifying the contact about how to install Windows Messenger (see Figure 3-15), click the Send E-mail button and enter any personal message in the resulting window.

8. Click Next and then click Cancel to close the wizard (or, if you click Next at this point, you begin the process all over again to add another contact).

Figure 3-14: The initial Windows Messenger window

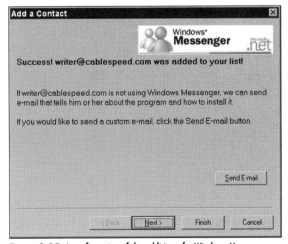

Figure 3-15: A confirmation of the addition of a Windows Messenger contact

Send an Instant Message in Windows Messenger

1. Choose Start⇨All Programs⇨Windows Messenger and sign in, if necessary.

2. In the Windows Messenger window shown in Figure 3-16, click a contact displayed in the Online list, and then click the Send an Instant Message link at the bottom of the window.

3. In the window shown in Figure 3-17, enter a message, and then click Send.

4. Now if your contact is online and replies, keep on chit-chatting to your heart's content. When you're done, click the Close button.

 You can do all sorts of things in Windows Messenger. For example, you can invite another person to the conversation, send a file or photo to the person you're chatting with, and use a whiteboard feature to keep notes or brainstorm with your friend.

Figure 3-16: The Windows Messenger window

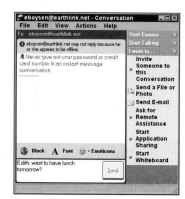

Figure 3-17: An instant messaging conversation in progress

Part II
Getting on the Internet

The 5th Wave   By Rich Tennant

THE SECRET ROOM AT EVERY
INTERNET SERVICE PROVIDER

KNOCK
FIRST

DISCONNECT

"I'll be right there. Let me just take care of
this user. He's about halfway through a
3 hour download."

Accessing the Internet

The Internet has become as integral to computing as lettuce to a salad. It's the way people communicate, transfer files, share images and music, shop for goods and services, and research everything from aardvarks to zebras.

Getting connected to the Internet isn't hard. Most Internet service providers (ISPs) provide software to set up your connection automatically. But you can connect in a few different ways, and you'll encounter a few different technologies. You might also need to tinker around with some settings to get things working just the way you want them to.

In this chapter, you find out how to make and manage Internet connections, including:

➡ **Setting up your connection:** A New Connection Wizard helps you with this process. Then you can designate your default connection so that you log on to the Internet the way you prefer.

➡ **Modifying settings:** Whether you use a TCP/IP or an always-on connection (such as cable or DSL), you discover the ins and outs of configuring them here, as well as how to share your Internet connection with someone else.

➡ **Using your Internet connection to connect to a network:** If you're like many people, you might need to tap into your workplace network from a remote location. It's easy to do, and I tell you how.

Chapter 4

Get ready to . . .

Set Up a New ISP Internet Connection

1. Choose Start⇨My Network Places.

2. In the resulting window, click the View Network Connections link.

3. In the resulting Network Connections window (see Figure 4-1), in the Network Tasks pane, click the Create a New Connection link.

4. In the New Connection Wizard dialog box, click Next.

5. In the resulting dialog box, accept the default selection of Connect to the Internet, and then click Next.

6. In the resulting New Connection Wizard, shown in Figure 4-2, select one of the following three options to set up a new ISP account:

   • The Choose from a List of Internet Service Providers (ISPs) option allows you to quickly set up MSN or choose from a list of other ISPs. Making this choice leads you to the Internet Connection Wizard, where your choices vary depending on the service provider you select.

   • If you have all the information about your ISP account and want to enter it manually, Set Up My Connection Manually is the choice for you.

   • The Use the CD I Got from My ISP option is pretty obvious. If you have a CD, whether an ISP sent it to you or you picked it up at the supermarket, select this option to activate the setup instructions for that ISP.

7. Click Next and follow the instructions to finish setting up your ISP connection. Note that you need to select the type of connection (for example, cable modem or dial-up) and create a user name and password for your new account during this process.

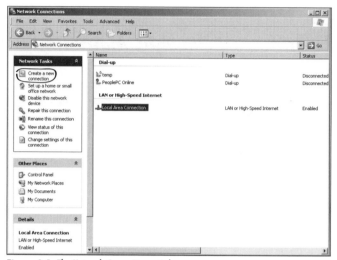

Figure 4-1: The Network Connections window

 In many cases, if you have a disc from your ISP, you don't need to follow these steps at all. Just pop that CD into your CD-ROM drive, and in no time a window appears and gives you instructions for setting up your account.

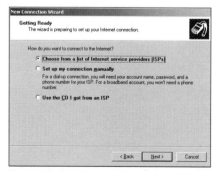

Figure 4-2: New Connection Wizard, Getting Ready dialog box

Set Up a Dial-Up Connection to an Existing ISP Account Manually

1. Choose Start⇨My Network Places.

2. In the My Network Places window, click the View Network Connections link.

3. In the Network Connections window under Network Tasks, click the Create a New Connection link.

4. In the New Connection Wizard dialog box, click Next.

5. In the resulting dialog box, accept the default selection of Connect to the Internet, and click Next.

6. In the resulting dialog box, select the Set Up My Connection Manually option, and click Next.

7. In the Internet Connection dialog box, shown in Figure 4-3, select the Connect Using a Dial-Up Modem option.

8. In the Internet Account Information (see Figure 4-4), enter this information:

   • Your ISP's name

   • The ISP's dial-up phone number

   • Your user name and password

   • Whether this is the default connection

   • Whether to use firewall protection for this connection

9. When the final wizard dialog box appears, click Finish to create the connection.

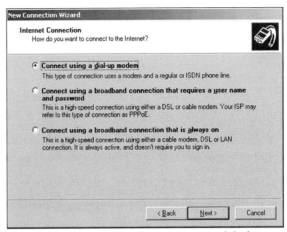

Figure 4-3: New Connection Wizard, Internet Connection dialog box

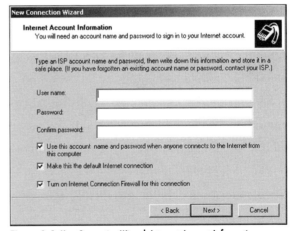

Figure 4-4: New Connection Wizard, Internet Account Information dialog box

Share an Internet Connection on a Network

1. Choose Start⇨My Network Places.

2. In the resulting My Network Places window, click the View Network Connections link.

3. In the resulting Network Connections window (see Figure 4-5), click a connection to select it, and then click the Change Settings of This Connection link.

4. In the resulting Properties dialog box (the name of the dialog box is the name of your Internet service provider), click the Advanced tab.

5. Select the check box labeled Allow Other Network Users to Connect through This Computer's Internet Connection (see Figure 4-6).

6. If you want to dial this connection automatically when another computer on your network tries to access it, select the Establish a Dial-Up Connection whenever a Computer on My Network Attempts to Access the Internet check box.

7. If you want other people on your network to control the shared Internet connection by enabling or disabling it, select the Allow Other Network Users to Control or Disable the Shared Internet Connection check box.

8. In the Internet Connection Sharing area of the Earthlink Properties dialog box, in the Home Networking Connection, select any adapter that connects the computer that shares an Internet connection to other computers on your network.

9. Click OK twice to save the shared connection settings.

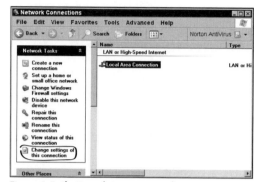

Figure 4-5: The Network Connections window

 Users on your network also have to make some settings to use your shared connection. They have to configure TCP/IP settings on their local area connections so that they get an IP connection automatically.

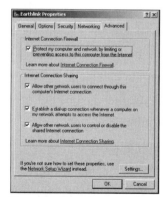

Figure 4-6: Selected options in the Properties dialog box

Configure a TCP/IP Connection

1. Choose Start➪My Network Places.

2. In the resulting My Network Places window, click the View Network Connections link.

3. Click the connection that you want to set up and then click Change Settings of this Connection.

4. In the resulting Earthlink Properties dialog box (the name of the dialog box is the name of your Internet service provider), display the Networking tab (see Figure 4-7).

5. On the Networking tab, in the This Connection Uses the Following Items area, select the Internet Properties (TCP/IP) option, and then click the Properties button.

6. In the Internet Protocol (TCP/IP) Properties dialog box that appears, shown in Figure 4-8, to allow addresses to be assigned automatically, select the Obtain an IP Address Automatically option, and then click OK twice.

 Although you can enter addresses manually in the Internet Protocol (TCP/IP) Properties dialog box, I recommend letting them be assigned automatically. Then if there's a change in your setup, you don't have to go in and manually modify addresses. This also saves you the hassle of having to manually configure certain settings, such as the Domain Name Service, which implements the Domain Name System (DNS). Don't want to worry about such techie things? Me neither. That's why I just let addresses be assigned automatically.

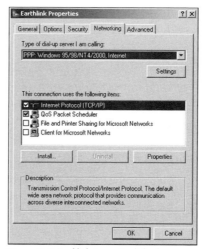

Figure 4-7: Earthlink Properties dialog box, Networking tab

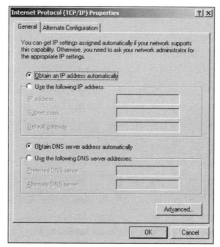

Figure 4-8: Internet Protocol (TCP/IP) Properties dialog box, General tab

Set Up an Always-On Connection

1. Choose Start⇨My Network Places.

2. In the My Network Places window, click the View Network Connections link.

3. In the Network Connections window under Network Tasks, click the Create a New Connection link.

4. In the New Connection Wizard dialog box, click Next.

5. In the resulting dialog box, accept the default selection of Connect to the Internet, and click Next.

6. In the Getting Ready dialog box, shown in Figure 4-9, select the Set Up My Connection Manually option and click Next.

7. In the Internet Connection dialog box, shown in Figure 4-10, select the Connect Using a Broadband Connection That Is Always On option and click Next.

8. In the following dialog boxes, the wizard notifies you that Windows will detect your connection and make settings for you. When you reach the final wizard dialog box, click Finish to complete the process.

 You might not have to do any of these steps to set up an always-on connection. If your provider doesn't require a user name and password to be entered, simply connect your broadband or cable modem, and then restart your computer. Windows should automatically detect the connection.

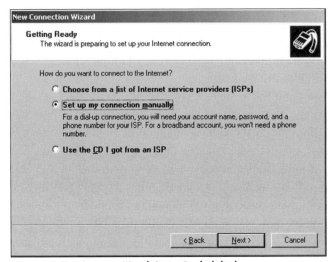

Figure 4-9: New Connection Wizard, Getting Ready dialog box

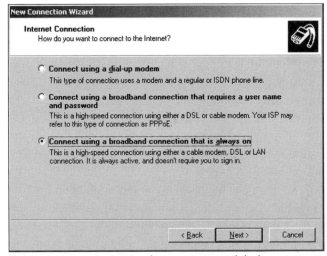

Figure 4-10: New Connection Wizard, Internet Connection dialog box

Set Up a Connection to the Network at Your Workplace

1. Choose Start⇨My Network Places.

2. In the resulting My Network Places window, click the View Network Connections link.

3. In the Network Connections window under Network Tasks, click the Create a New Connection link.

4. In the New Connection Wizard dialog box, click Next.

5. In the Network Connection Type dialog box shown in Figure 4-11, click the Connect to the Network at My Workplace radio button and then click Next.

6. In the resulting dialog box, choose either the Dial-Up Connection or Virtual Private Network Connection option, and then click Next.

7. In the next two dialog boxes, enter a name for the connection, and then complete one of two tasks:

   • For a dial-up connection, enter a phone number (see Figure 4-12).

   • For a VPN connection, select whether to automatically dial the initial connection.

8. When you reach the final wizard dialog box, click Finish to complete the wizard.

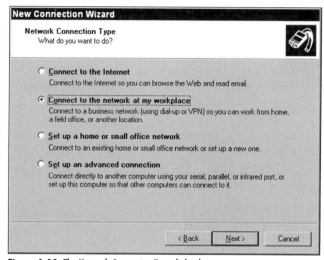

Figure 4-11: The Network Connection Type dialog box

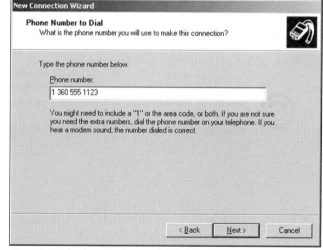

Figure 4-12: The Phone Number to Dial dialog box

Designate Your Default Connection

1. Choose Start⇨Control Panel.

2. In the Control Panel window, click the Network and Internet Connections link. In the resulting window (see Figure 4-13), click the Set Up or Change Your Internet Connection link.

3. In the resulting Internet Properties dialog box (see Figure 4-14) with the Connections tab displayed, click the connection that you want to make the default.

4. Click the Set Default button, and then click OK.

 Your computer uses the default connection anytime you click a link or open your browser. However, you can still manually open any connection by opening the Network Connections window, right-clicking any connection, and choosing Connect.

 If your default connection is through an external modem and you're having trouble getting online, check the obvious: Loose or incorrect connections to your modem can stop you from getting online.

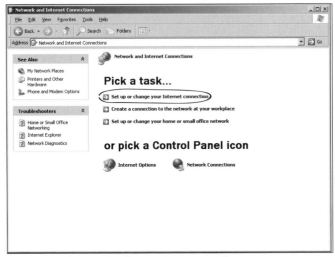

Figure 4-13: The Network and Internet Connections window

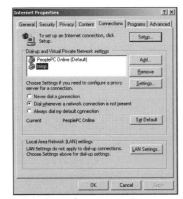

Figure 4-14: The Internet Properties dialog box, Connections tab

Remove an Internet Connection

1. Choose Start⇨Control Panel.

2. In the Control Panel window, click the Network and Internet Connections link.

3. In the Network and Internet Connections window (refer to Figure 4-13), click the Set up or change your Internet connection link.

4. In the resulting Internet Properties dialog box (see Figure 4-15) with the Connections tab displayed, click the connection that you want to delete and click the Remove button.

5. Click OK.

Repair a Connection

1. Choose Start⇨My Network Places.

2. In the My Network Place window, click the View Network Connections link.

3. In the Network Connections window (see Figure 4-16), right-click the connection and choose Repair.

 Sometimes repairing a connection doesn't do the trick. In that case it's best to delete the connection, and just create it again by clicking the Create a New Connection link in the Network Connections window and entering the correct settings.

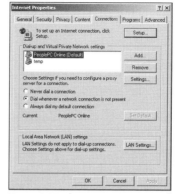

Figure 4-15: The Internet Properties window

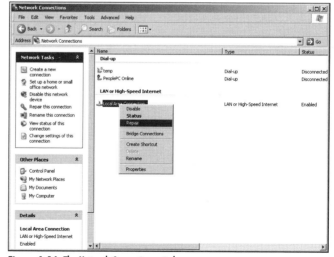

Figure 4-16: The Network Connections window

Browsing the Web with Internet Explorer

*T*o drive around the Internet superhighway, you need a good vehicle. A *browser* is a program that you can use to get around the Internet, and Internet Explorer (IE) is one of the best.

IE is built into Windows because it's made by Microsoft, so the Microsoft folks can put it anywhere they like. This is good news for you because by using IE you can

➡ **Navigate all around the Web:** Use the IE navigation features to jump from one site to another, go back to places you've been (via the Favorites and History features), and search for new places to visit.

➡ **Download files to your computer or print:** When you find what you want online, such as a graphic image or free software program, you might want to save it to your computer for future use. Do you need a hard copy of what you've found? Just use the Print feature of IE.

➡ **Protect yourself:** The Internet is a bit dangerous — a place where some people try to get at your private information and make nefarious use of it. IE provides privacy settings and special features to control the use of *cookies* (small files that folks who run Web sites insert on your hard drive to help them track your online activities). You can use the Content Advisor to limit the online locations that your computer can visit.

Get ready to . . .

Navigate the Web

1. Open IE by double-clicking the Internet Explorer icon on the Windows desktop.

2. Enter a Web site address in the Address Bar (www.pubstudio.com is my company's Web site) and click Go, as shown in Figure 5-1.

    Figure 5-1 shows a button for the Norton AntiVirus program. Though not a default IE button, some antivirus programs might add such tools. I highly recommend that you use an antivirus program if you navigate the Web frequently.

3. On the resulting Web site, click a link or enter another address to proceed to another page.

    A link can be an icon or text. A text link is identifiable by colored text, usually blue or purple. After you click a link, it usually changes color to show that it's been followed before.

4. Click the Back button to move back to the first page that you visited. Click the Forward button to go forward to the second page that you visited.

5. Click the down-pointing arrow at the far right of the Address Bar to display a list of sites that you visited recently, as shown in Figure 5-2. Click a site in this list to go there.

    The Stop and Refresh buttons on the Standard toolbar are useful for navigating sites. Clicking the Stop button stops a page that's loading. So, if you made a mistake entering the address, or if the page is taking longer than you'd like to load, click the Stop button to halt the process. Clicking the Refresh button redisplays the current page. This is especially useful if a page updates information frequently, such as on a stock market site. You can also use the Refresh button if a page doesn't load correctly; it might load correctly when refreshed.

Figure 5-1: MSN.com, the IE default home page

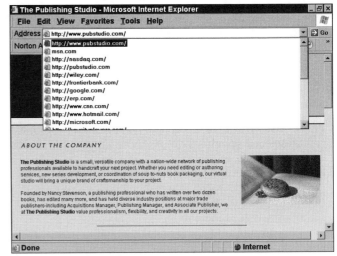

Figure 5-2: Recently visited sites

Search the Web

1. Open IE and click the Search button on the Standard toolbar.

2. In the resulting Search pane, make sure that the Find a Web Page option is selected, and then enter a search term in the text box. Click Go.

3. In the resulting list of links or thumbnail pictures (depending on settings), click a link to go to that Web page. If you don't see the link that you need, and more than one page of results is displayed, scroll down — if necessary — to click the link labeled Next to move to the next page.

4. Click the New button at the top of the Search pane to clear the search term, and then enter a new search term.

5. Click the Customize button to set your search options.

6. In the resulting Customize Search Settings dialog box, shown in Figure 5-3, select one of the following options, and then click OK to apply it:

   - **Use Search Assistant:** Select this option and then select the categories that you want to use to search. After you click OK, your new categories are displayed in the Search pane.

   - **Use One Search Service:** Select this option and then select a search service, such as Yahoo!, Lycos, or Excite, from the list that appears. Click OK, and that search service becomes the default engine for the Search pane.

     Figure 5-4 shows the results of selecting MSN as the search service, entering the *natural English* question, **What is the capital of Brazil?**, and clicking Go.

   - **Use Search Companion:** Select this option and refine your search by specifying items or locations.

Figure 5-3: The Customize Search Settings dialog box

 Knowing how search engines work can save you time. For example, if you search by entering **golden retriever**, you typically get sites that contain both words or either word. If you put a plus sign between these two keywords (*golden+retriever*), you get only sites that contain both words.

Figure 5-4: Search Companion results displayed

Find Content on a Web Page

1. With IE open and the Web page that you want to search displayed, choose Edit⇨Find (on This Page).

2. In the resulting dialog box, shown in Figure 5-5, enter the word that you want to search for. Use the following options to narrow your results:

   - **Match whole word only:** Select this option if you want to find only the whole word (for example, if you enter **cat** and want to find only *cat* and not *catatonic* or *catastrophe*).

   - **Match case:** Select this option if you want to match the case (for example, if you enter **Catholic** and want to find only the always-capitalized religion and not the adjective *catholic*).

3. In the Direction area, select Up if you want to search the beginning of the page first; select Down if you want the end of the page searched first.

4. Click the Find Next button. The first instance of the word is highlighted on the page (see Figure 5-6). If you want to find another instance, click the Find Next button again.

5. When you're done searching, click the Cancel button in the Find dialog box.

 Many Web sites, such as www.littleriverpetshop.com, have a Search This Site feature that allows you to search not only the displayed Web page, but all Web pages on a Web site. Look for a Search text box and make sure that it searches the site and not the entire Internet.

Figure 5-5: The Find dialog box

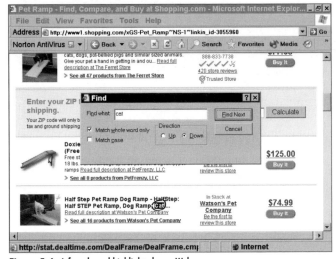

Figure 5-6: A found word highlighted on a Web page

Set Up a Home Page

1. Open IE and choose Tools⇨Internet Options.

2. In the resulting Internet Options dialog box, on the General tab, enter a Web site address to use as your home page, as shown in Figure 5-7, and click OK.

   (My company's home page is shown in Figure 5-8 — pretty, isn't it?) Alternatively, click one of the following preset option buttons, as shown in Figure 5-7:

   • **Use Current:** Sets whatever page is currently displayed in the browser window as your home page.

   • **Use Default:** This setting sends you to the MSN Web page.

   • **Use Blank:** If you're a minimalist, this setting is for you. No Web page displays, just a blank area.

3. Click the Home Page icon to go to your home page.

 What makes a good home page? Well, if you absolutely always check the news when you first log on, how about a news site, such as www.cnn.com? Or if you spend a lot of time online researching a topic, select a site with links to information about that topic (www.genealogy.com, for example). Just want a fun jumping off point for the whole Internet? Online provider sites, such as www.msn.com or www.yahoo.com, often provide customizable home pages that let you include topics of interest to you, such as horoscopes, news, local weather, shopping links, or sports.

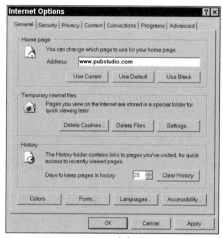

Figure 5-7: Internet Options dialog box

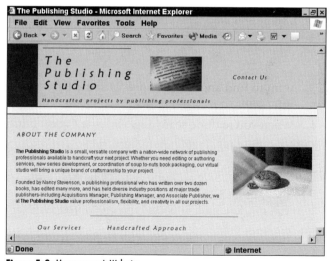

Figure 5-8: My company's Web site

Add a Web Site to Favorites

1. Open IE, enter the URL of a Web site that you want to add to your Favorites list, and click Go.

2. Choose Favorites⇨Add to Favorites.

3. In the resulting Add Favorite dialog box, shown in Figure 5-9, modify the name of the Favorite listing to something easily recognizable. Click OK to add the site.

4. You can go to a favorite site in a couple different ways:

   • Choose the Favorites menu and then click the name of the site from the list that's displayed.

   • Click the Favorites button on the Standard toolbar, and your favorites are displayed in the Favorites pane (see Figure 5-10). Click one to go there.

 Regularly cleaning out your Favorites list is a good idea — after all, do you really need the sites that you used to plan last year's vacation? Choose Favorites⇨Organize Favorites. In the resulting dialog box, click a site to select it, and then rename it, delete it, or move it.

Organize Favorites

1. With Internet Explorer open, choose Favorites⇨Organize Favorites.

2. In the resulting Organize Favorites dialog box (see Figure 5-11), click the Create Folder, Rename, Move to Folder, or Delete buttons to organize your favorites.

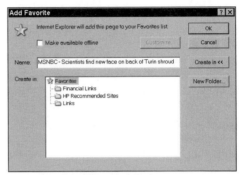

Figure 5-9: The Add Favorite dialog box

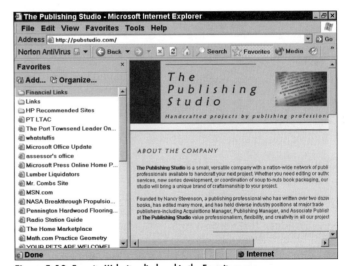

Figure 5-10: Favorite Web sites displayed in the Favorites pane

3. With a favorite Web page highlighted, select the Make Available Offline check box (that appears in the text box below the buttons) to view the last displayed version of the Web page even after you log off of your Internet connection.

4. When you finish organizing your Favorites, click Close.

 These steps provide a handy way to manage several sites or folders, but you can also organize favorite sites one by one by using the Favorites pane. (You display the Favorites pane by clicking the Favorites button on the Standard toolbar.) Right-click any favorite site listed in the pane and choose a command: Create New Folder, Delete, Rename, or Make Available Offline. You can also reorganize folders in the Favorites pane by dragging the icons up or down in the list.

View Your Browsing History

1. Choose View⇨Explorer Bar⇨History to display sites you've previously visited.

2. In the resulting History pane, click the arrow on the View button to show all viewing options. (The default view is By Date.)

3. With the By Date view selected (as shown in Figure 5-12), click one of the folders in the list to display all sites in a particular category, such as the Last Week or 2 Weeks Ago folders. If you want to revisit a site in the list, click it, and you're there.

 To clear the IE History feature, choose Tools⇨Internet Options. On the General tab, click the Clear History button. To change how many days of searching the History feature saves, on the General tab, change the Days to Keep Pages in History setting by clicking the up or down spinner arrows. You can also delete a single site or folder from the History pane by right-clicking it and choosing Delete.

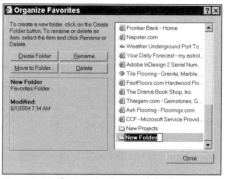

Figure 5-11: The Organize Favorites dialog box

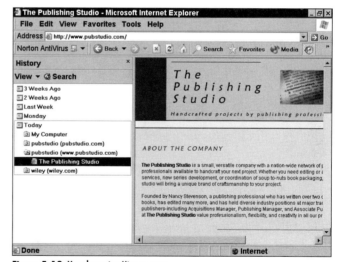

Figure 5-12: Your browsing History pane

Customize Internet Explorer

1. Open IE.

2. In the resulting default home page (www.msn.com, shown in Figure 15-13), customize your page as follows:

   - **Select text size:** Choose View⇨Text Size and select the size that you want displayed.

   - **Personalize the Explorer Bar:** Choose View⇨Explorer Bar and choose an item from the list that you want to view in the Explorer Bar area on the left side of the IE screen, as shown in Figure 5-14.

 Displaying the History pane in the Explorer Bar is useful, but here's a shortcut for visiting recently viewed sites: You can find Web pages that you've visited (up to nine of them) by clicking the arrow to the side of the Back button and choosing one from the list that's displayed.

   - **Add Toolbars:** Choose View⇨Toolbars. Try out all the toolbars in the list to see which ones you want to display. (Figure 5-14 shows all available toolbars displayed. Note that you can also include any third-party toolbars you might have added. For example, you can add the Google Toolbar to IE by downloading it from www.google.com.)

 You can resize the various panes of Internet Explorer, such as the main Web page view pane and Explorer Bar. Move your mouse over the vertical divider between panes until the cursor becomes a line with arrows on both ends, and then click and drag the divider to enlarge or shrink a pane.

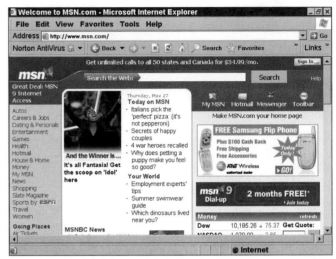

Figure 5-13: The default home page

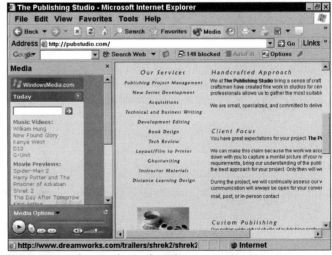

Figure 5-14: Explorer Bar showing the Media pane

Download Files

1. Open a Web site that contains downloadable files. Some Web sites offer a Download Now button, but others provide a link to download a file.

2. Click the appropriate link to proceed.

3. In the resulting File Download dialog box, shown in Figure 5-15, choose either option:

   - **Click Open to download to a temporary folder.** You can run an installation program for software, for example. However, beware: If you run a program directly from the Internet, you could be introducing dangerous viruses to your system. You might want to set up an antivirus program to scan files before downloading them.

   - **Click Save to save the file to your hard drive.** In the Save As dialog box, select the folder on your computer or removable storage media (a CD-ROM, for example) where you want to save the file. If you're downloading software, you need to locate the downloaded file and click it to run the installation.

 Click Cancel in the File Download dialog box if you're worried that the file might be unsafe to download.

Change Privacy Settings

1. With IE open, choose Tools⇨Internet Options and click the Privacy tab, as shown in Figure 5-16.

2. Click the slider and drag it up or down to make different levels of security settings.

3. Read the choices and select a setting that suits you. Click OK to save it.

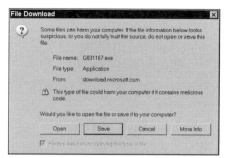

Figure 5-15: The File Download dialog box

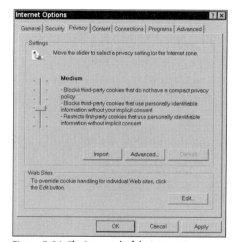

Figure 5-16: The Privacy tab of the Internet Options dialog box

 The default Privacy setting is Medium and is probably a good bet for most people. To restore the default setting, click the Default button in the Internet Options dialog box Privacy sheet or use the slider to move back to Medium.

Enable Content Advisor

1. With IE open, choose Tools⇨Internet Options.

2. In the resulting Internet Options dialog box, click the Content tab to display it.

3. Click the Enable button. (*Note:* If there is no Enable button but Disable and Settings buttons instead, Content Advisor is already enabled. Click the Settings button to see the options and make changes if you wish.)

4. In the Content Advisor dialog box (see Figure 5-17) on the Ratings tab, click one of the four options: Language, Nudity, Sex, or Violence. Use the slider to set the site-screening level that's appropriate for you.

5. Repeat Step 4 for each of the categories.

6. Click the Approved Sites tab (see Figure 5-18) and enter the name of a specific site that you want to control access to. Then click either of the following options:

   • **Always:** Allows users to view the site, even if it's included in the Content Advisor screening level you've set.

   • **Never:** Means that nobody can visit the site even if it's acceptable to Content Advisor.

7. When you finish making your settings, click OK twice to save them.

 If you want to view sites that you don't want others to see, you can do that, too. On the General tab of the Content Advisor dialog box, make sure that the Supervisor Can Type a Password to Allow Viewers to View Restricted Content check box is selected, and then click Create Password. In the dialog box that appears, enter the password, confirm it, and then enter a hint and click OK. Now if you're logged on as the system administrator, you can get to any restricted site by using this password.

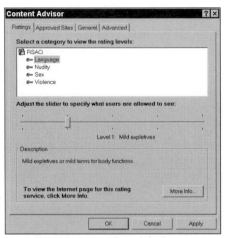

Figure 5-17: The Content Advisor dialog box

Figure 5-18: The Approved Sites tab of the Content Advisor

Print a Web Page

1. If a Web page includes a link or button to print or display a print version of a page, click that and follow the instructions.

2. If the page doesn't include a link for printing, simply press Ctrl+P.

3. In the resulting Print dialog box, decide how much of the document you want to print and click one of the options in the Page Range area, as shown in Figure 5-19.

 Note that choosing Current Page or entering page numbers in the Pages text box of the Print dialog box doesn't mean much when printing a Web page — the whole document might print because Web pages aren't divided into pages the way that word processing documents are.

4. Click the up arrow in the Number of Copies text box to print multiple copies. If you want multiple copies collated, select the Collate check box.

5. When you've adjusted all settings, click Print.

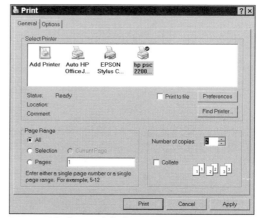

Figure 5-19: The Print dialog box

Exchanging E-Mail with Outlook Express

Chapter

6

*O*nce upon a time, people chatted around the water cooler or over lunch, but that's all changed now. Now the place to spend your time communicating is online.

E-mail is the cornerstone of online communication. You've probably sent an e-mail (unless you were brought up by wolves in the forest), but you might not be familiar with the ins and outs of using Outlook Express, the miniversion of the Outlook e-mail program from Microsoft that's built into Windows XP.

To make your e-mailing life easy, this chapter takes a look at these tasks:

➡ **Receive, send, and forward messages:** Deal with the ins and outs of receiving and sending mail. Use the formatting tools that Outlook Express provides to make your messages pretty.

➡ **Add information into the Address Book:** You can quickly and easily manage your contacts and organize the messages you save in e-mail folders.

➡ **Set up the layout of all Outlook Express features:** Use the Folder Bar and Layout features to create the most efficient workspace.

➡ **Manage your e-mail account:** Set up an e-mail account and create, modify, and add rules for your account to operate by.

Get ready to . . .

Open Outlook and Receive Messages

1. Choose Start➪Outlook Express.

2. In the Outlook Express window, press Ctrl+M to send and receive all messages.

3. Click the Inbox item in the Folders list to view messages. New messages sport a small closed envelope icon; those with attachments have a paperclip icon as well (see Figure 6-1).

If you want to organize messages in the Inbox, you can do so by clicking any of the headings at the top, such as From to sort the messages alphabetically by sender, Received to sort by the date they were received, and so on.

If you have Windows XP Service Pack 2 installed, you will be alerted about attachments that might be harmful. In addition, pictures in e-mails might be blocked from downloading to your computer; you can click a red X labeled Click Here to Download Pictures to have them appear in the e-mail. See Chapter 12 for more about Outlook Express and SP2.

Create and Send E-Mail

1. Choose Start➪Outlook Express.

2. Click the Create Mail button on the Outlook toolbar to create a new blank e-mail form (see Figure 6-2).

3. Type the e-mail address of the recipient in the To text box and enter an address in the Cc text box to send a copy of the message.

4. Click in the Subject text box and type a concise yet descriptive subject.

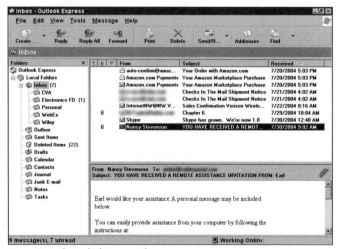

Figure 6-1: The Outlook Express Inbox

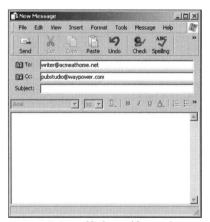

Figure 6-2: A new, blank e-mail form with addresses entered

5. Click in the message window and type your message (see Figure 6-3).

6. When you finish typing your message, it's a good idea to spell check it (unless you're the regional state spelling champ). Click the Spelling button; if there's possible misspelling, the word is highlighted, and the Spelling dialog box appears (see Figure 6-4). At this point you have some choices:

- Click the Ignore button to ignore this instance of the misspelling.

- Click the Ignore All button to ignore all instances.

- Click a suggested alternate spelling and click the Change button to change that instance, or click the Change All button to change all instances of the word.

- Click the Add button to add the current spelling of the word to the Spelling feature dictionary so it's never questioned again.

- Click the Send button. The message is on its way!

 If the message is really urgent, you might also click the Priority button to add a bright red exclamation mark to the message header to alert the recipient. Click twice more to return the priority to low.

 Remember that when creating an e-mail you can address it to a stored address by using the Address Book feature. Click the To button and your Address Book appears. You can then select a contact from there. Outlook Express also allows you to just begin to type a stored contact in an address field (To or Cc) and it fills in likely options as you type. When it fills in the correct name, just press Enter to select it.

Figure 6-3: A message typed and ready to go

Figure 6-4: The Spelling dialog box

Send an Attachment

1. Create a new e-mail message, address it, and enter a subject.

2. Click the Attach button.

3. In the Insert Attachment dialog box that appears (see Figure 6-5), locate the document that you want by using the Look In drop-down list and the File Name text box and then click Attach.

4. With the name of the attached file now in the Attach text box (see Figure 6-6), type a message (or not — after all, a picture *is* worth a thousand words).

5. Click the Send button to send.

 If you want to send somebody your own contact information, create a business card in your Address Book and attach it to an e-mail. This is saved in vCard format, and the recipient can then import it into his or her Address Book. Just create yourself as a contact, and then in the Address Book window choose File↑Export↑Business Card, and save it. Now you can attach it to any e-mail, any time.

 Some e-mail programs limit the size of a message and its attachment, so a larger attachment just might not get through. To change the size of messages you can send, choose Tools⇨Accounts and on the Mail tab click Properties. On the Advanced tab, select Break Apart Messages Larger Than X and enter the maximum file size your e-mail server can accommodate.

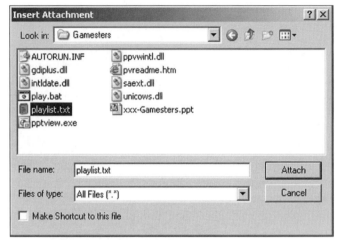

Figure 6-5: The Insert Attachment dialog box

Figure 6-6: The Attach field showing an attached file

Read a Message

1. Double-click an e-mail message in your Inbox. Unread messages sport an icon of an unopened envelope to the left of the message subject.

2. Use the scrollbars in the message window to scroll down through the message and read it (see Figure 6-7).

3. If the message has an attachment, it is shown as a paper-clip symbol when the message is closed in your Inbox; attachments are listed in the Attach box in the open message. To open an attachment, double-click it.

4. In the Open Attachment Warning dialog box (see Figure 6-8), click the Open radio button, and then click OK. The attachment opens in whatever program is associated with it (such as the Windows Fax and Picture Viewer for a graphics file) or the program it was created in (such as Word for Windows).

 If you'd rather save an attachment to a storage disk or your hard drive, when the Open Attachment Warning dialog box opens, click the Save As radio button, and in the Save As dialog box that appears, choose a location and provide a name for the file and then click Save.

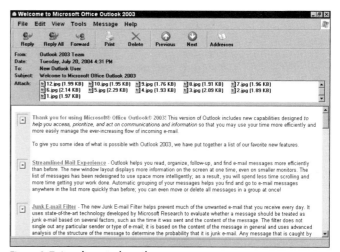

Figure 6-7: A newly received e-mail message

Figure 6-8: The Open Attachment Warning dialog box

Reply to a Message

1. With the message you want to reply to open, select one of the following reply options:

    *   **Reply:** Send the reply to only the author.

    *   **Reply All:** Send a reply to the author as well as everyone who received the original message.

 Click the Next or Previous buttons on the toolbar to move from one e-mail to the other in the order they're listed in your Inbox.

2. In the resulting e-mail form (see Figure 6-9), enter a new recipient(s) in the To and/or Cc text boxes and type your message in the message window area.

3. Click the Send button to send the reply.

 If you don't want that to include the original message in your reply, choose Tools⇨Options and click the Send tab. Deselect the check box labeled Include Message in Reply, and then click OK.

Forward E-Mail Messages

1. Open the e-mail message that you want to forward.

2. Click the Forward button on the toolbar.

3. In the message that appears with Fw: added to the beginning of the subject line, enter a new recipient(s) in the To and Cc fields, and enter any message that you want to include in the message window area, as shown in the example in Figure 6-10.

4. Click Send to forward the message.

Figure 6-9: Add your message

Figure 6-10: A message ready to be forwarded

Create and Add a Signature

1. Choose Tools⇨Options to open the Options dialog box. Click the Signatures tab (see Figure 6-11).

2. Click the New button to create a new signature and enter the Signatures text.

3. Select the Add Signatures to All Outgoing Messages check box and make sure that the signature is selected as the default. (*Note:* Select the Don't Add Signatures to Replies and Forwards check box to insert a signature manually. If you want to add the signature only occasionally, I suggest you go this route.)

4. Click OK to save the signature. To manually add a signature to an open e-mail message, choose Insert⇨Signature and select a signature from the list that appears to insert it (see Figure 6-12).

 If you have different e-mail accounts and want to assign a different signature to each one, when you're on the Signatures tab of the Options dialog box, select a signature in the Signatures list box, and click the Advanced button. Then select an account to associate it with.

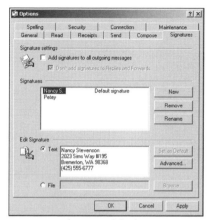

Figure 6-11: The Options dialog box, Signatures tab

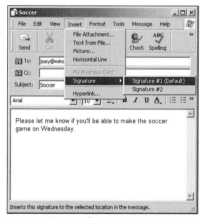

Figure 6-12: Manually inserting a signature in an e-mail

Format E-Mail Messages

1. Create a new e-mail message or open a message and click Reply or Forward.

2. Select the text that you want to format (see Figure 6-13).

3. Use any of the following options to make changes to the font (see the toolbar containing these tools in Figure 6-13, and a message with various formats applied in Figure 6-14):

   - **Font box arrow drop-down list:** Select an option in the drop-down list to apply it to the text.

   - **Font Size drop-down list:** Change the font size.

   - **Paragraph Style button:** Apply a preset style, such as Heading 1 or Address.

   - **Bold, Italic, or Underline buttons:** Apply styles to selected text.

   - **Font Color button:** Display a color palette and click a color to apply it to selected text.

   - **Formatting Numbers or Formatting Bullets buttons:** Apply numbering order to lists or precede each item with a round bullet.

   - **Align Left, Center, Align Right, or Justify buttons:** Adjust the alignment.

   - **Increase Indentation or Decrease Indentation button:** Indent that paragraph to the right or move it to the left.

   - **Insert Horizontal Line button:** Add a line to your message.

Figure 6-13 : Text selected for formatting

Figure 6-14: A variety of formats applied to an e-mail message

Add Stationery

1. Click the arrow on the Create button in the Outlook Express main window and select a stationery option listed in the menu that appears, or choose the Select Stationery command to get more choices.

2. In the Select Stationery dialog box that appears (see Figure 6-15), select a stationery from the list.

3. Click OK to apply the stationery to the new message.

4. With a new, reply, or forwarded message open, you can apply stationery by using either of these methods:

   • Choose Format➪Apply Stationery, and then click a stationery to apply (see Figure 6-16).

   • Choose More Stationery to access the Select Stationery dialog box.

 You can also insert a picture in an e-mail. With the e-mail form open, choose Insert➪Picture. Locate a picture by clicking the Browse button, choose an alignment for the picture in the body of the e-mail message, and click OK.

 If you have applied stationery and decide that you don't want to use it anymore, just click the arrow on the Create button and select No Stationery from the drop-down menu.

Figure 6-15: The Select Stationery dialog box

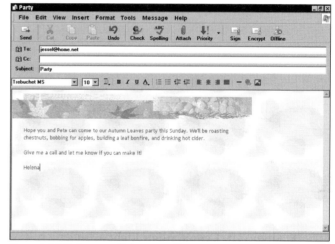

Figure 6-16: Stationery applied to an e-mail message

Add Contacts to the Address Book

1. In the Outlook Express main window, click the Addresses button to open the Address Book window.

2. To create a new contact in the resulting Address Book window, shown in Figure 6-17, click the New button and select New Contact from the menu that appears. (*Note:* New Group can be used to create a group of people from existing contacts, such as your car pool members.)

3. In the resulting Properties dialog box, shown in Figure 6-18, you select from the go to the following options tabs to enter contact information:

   • **Name tab:** Enter the person's name and e-mail address. (This is the only information you must enter to create a contact.)

   • **Home tab:** Enter the person's home address, phone, fax, cell phone, and Web site.

   • **Business tab:** Enter information about the company that the person works for, job title, pager, and even a map to help you find his or her office.

   • **Personal tab:** Enter the person's family members' names, as well as his or her gender, birthday, or anniversary.

   • **Other:** Use this space for miscellaneous notes.

   • **NetMeeting:** Insert information about the person's conferencing server if you meet online by using Microsoft's NetMeeting.

   • **Digital IDs:** Ensure secure communications. Digital IDs are certificates that you can use to verify the identity of the person with whom you're communicating.

4. Click OK to save your new contact information, and close the Address Book.

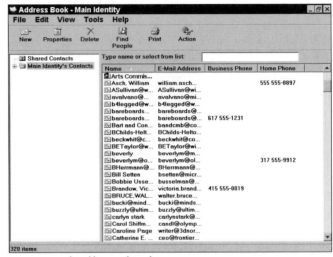

Figure 6-17: The Address Book window

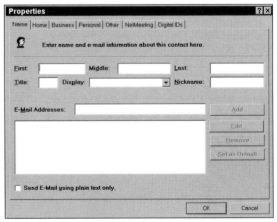

Figure 6-18: The Properties dialog box

Customize the Outlook Express Window Layout

1. Choose View⯈Layout to open the Window Layout Properties dialog box.

2. Click in various check boxes in the Basic section, as shown in Figure 6-19, to select items to display in separate panes (see Figure 6-20), including:

   - **Contacts:** A list of all the contacts in your Address Book; click any to address a new or forwarded message.

   - **Folder Bar:** A bar near the top of the screen that includes a drop-down list of folders.

   - **Folder List:** A pane containing a list of all folders.

   - **Outlook Bar:** This vertical bar includes icons for accessing your Inbox, Outbox, Sent Items, Deleted Items, and Drafts.

   - **Status Bar:** The bar across the bottom of screen that lists the number of messages in all your folders and the number of unread messages.

   - **Toolbar:** The bar containing tools you use to create and work with messages, such as Create, Reply, Forward, and Print.

   - **Views Bar:** A bar under the toolbar containing a drop-down menu with three commands: Hide Read Messages, Hide Read or Ignored Messages, and Show All Messages.

3. Select various options in the Preview Pane section to preview a message selected in the Inbox, Outbox, Drafts, Sent Items, or Deleted Items folders.

4. Click OK to apply and save all your layout settings.

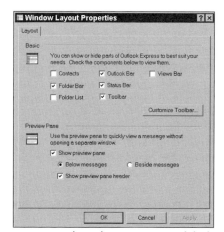

Figure 6-19: The Window Layout Properties dialog box

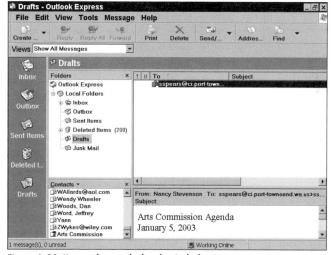

Figure 6-20: Various elements displayed in Outlook Express

Create Message Folders

1. Choose View⇨Layout to open the Window Layout Properties dialog box.

2. Click in their respective check boxes to select the Folder List and Folder bar, so you can view them and then click OK. Display the Folder List and Folder Bar.

3. In the Folder List, click a plus sign to the left of any folder to display its contents (see Figure 6-21).

4. Choose File⇨New⇨Folder.

5. In the resulting Create Folder dialog box (see Figure 6-22), select the folder that you want the new folder to be created in and enter a new folder name.

6. Click OK.

 Typically, you select the Local Folders item in Step 5 so that the new folder is at the same level as the Inbox, Outbox, and so on. Alternatively, you could select the Inbox item to place the new folder within the Inbox folder.

 Don't rely on messages stored in Outlook folders as your main storage space. Should you have serious Windows problems, it is more likely that you can restore files stored in Windows folders than those stored in Outlook.

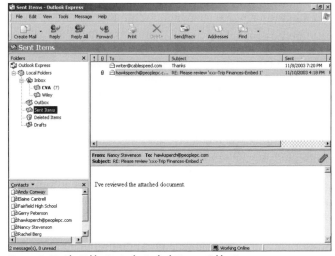

Figure 6-21: The Folder List in the Outlook Express Folder Bar

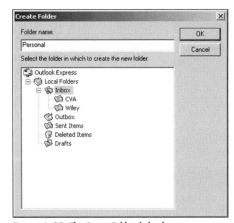

Figure 6-22: The Create Folder dialog box

Organize Messages in Folders

1. In the Folder List, click a plus sign to the left of any folder to display its contents (see Figure 6-23).

2. To place a message in a folder, you can do one of these actions:

- With a folder such as the Inbox displayed, click a message and drag it into a folder in the Folder List.

- With an e-mail message open, choose File➪Move to Folder or Copy to Folder. In the dialog box that appears (see Figure 6-24), select the appropriate folder and click OK.

- Right-click a message in a displayed folder and select choose Move to Folder or Copy to Folder. In the dialog box that appears, select the appropriate folder and click OK.

3. To delete a message display the folder it's saved to, select it, and click the Delete button or press Delete.

 If you try to delete a message from your Deleted Items folder, a message will appears asking if you if whether you really want to delete this message permanently. That's because when you delete a message from another folder, it's really not deleted, it's simply placed in the Deleted Items folder. To send it into oblivion, you have to delete it from the Deleted Items folder, confirming your deletion so that Outlook Express is really convinced that you mean what you say.

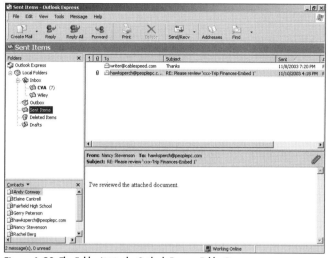

Figure 6-23: The Folder List in the Outlook Express Folder Bar

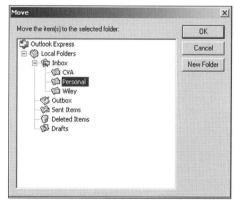

Figure 6-24: The Move dialog box

Manage an E-Mail Account

1. In the Outlook Express main window, choose Tools➪ Accounts.

2. In the resulting Internet Accounts dialog box, shown in Figure 6-25, set up a new account by clicking one of the following tabs:

   • **Mail:** For e-mail accounts.

   • **News:** For newsgroups.

   • **Directory Service:** For online search services used by the Address Book to search for people.

3. Click the Add button and choose the appropriate service.

4. In the resulting Internet Connection Wizard (see Figure 6-26), follow the setup steps.

5. To remove an account, click the Remove button on any of the tabs. A confirming message appears. To delete the account, click Yes.

6. Select an account and click the Set As Default button to make it the account that Windows connects you to when you go online. In the case of the mail server, the default is the one used to send any message.

7. When you finish setting up accounts, click the Close button to close the Internet Accounts dialog box.

 You'll be glad to hear that if you've installed Service Pack 2, it has a feature that prevents others from validating your e-mail address without your knowledge. If somebody tries to download something when you open your e-mail (that something is often a file that allows the sender to get an automatic reply from active e-mail accounts), you are alerted and offered the option of not allowing the download.

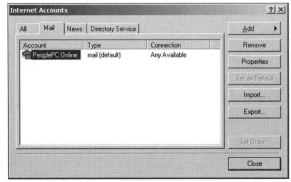

Figure 6-25: The Internet Accounts dialog box

 Following the Internet Connection Wizard often requires that you provide certain information about your Internet service provider (ISP), such as their mail server or connection method. Keep this information handy!

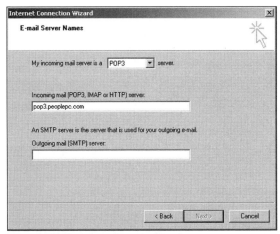

Figure 6-26: The Internet Connection Wizard

Create Mail Rules

1. Choose Tools⇨Message Rules⇨Mail.

2. In the resulting New Mail Rule dialog box (see Figure 6-27), click in a check box to set a Condition for the rule (for example, all messages Where the Subject Line Contains Specific Words, such as Sale or Free).

3. Click in a check box to select an Action for the rule. In the example in Step 2, for instance, you would select the Move It To The Specified Folder option.

4. In the Rule Description area, click the link (the colored text, such as Contains Specific Words). Fill in the specific information for the rule in the dialog box that appears (see Figure 6-28 for an example, where you enter the word **sale** to move e-mail with that word in the subject to another folder).

5. Fill in the Name of the Rule text box with a name that you can recognize, and then click OK.

After you create a rule, open the Message Rules dialog box by choosing Tools⇨Message Rules⇨Mail and then clicking Cancel. Click the Modify button in the Message dialog box to make changes to the rule, or click the Remove button to delete it.

Here are some rules that people find handy to create: Place messages marked as priority in a Priority folder, or put messages with attachments in an Attachments folder. When you're on vacation, choose to have all messages forwarded to somebody else, such as an assistant; or if a message is from a certain person, mark it with a color. *Note:* If you use the autoforward feature, you have to leave your computer on and leave Outlook Express open while you're away.

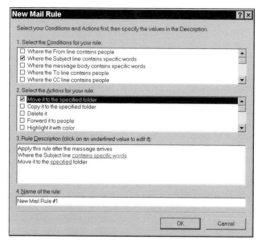

Figure 6-27: Specify rule details

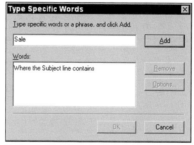

Figure 6-28: Add a specific description

Part III

Setting Up Hardware and Maintaining Your System

The 5th Wave   By Rich Tennant

"Drive carefully, remember your lunch, and always make a backup of your directory tree before modifying your hard drive partition file."

Setting Up New Hardware

Chapter 7

*P*eripherals, graphics cards, modems, SCSI (pronounced *skuzzy*, if you please) — just what the heck is all this stuff?

Collectively these items belong to the category of *computer hardware*. Your CPU and monitor are hardware. So are the cards slotted into your CPU that provide memory to run software and the mechanisms for playing sounds and videos. Printers are hardware, as is anything else that plugs into your computer.

It used to be that installing a new piece of hardware was a great occasion for groaning and moaning. Nothing was compatible, everything installed differently, and Windows itself didn't have much in the way of popular *drivers* (software that runs various pieces of hardware) ready and waiting. That's all changed with a technology called Plug and Play, which automates the installation process and some standardizing of connections through Universal Serial Bus (USB) ports. Windows now comes with a full framework of drivers for hardware devices, and whatever it doesn't have is usually easy to download from any hardware manufacturer's Web site. In this chapter, you find out how you can:

→ **Install and set up common peripherals:** Peripherals include a monitor, printer, and modem.

→ **Install and set up cards that slot into your CPU:** Add sound, video, and add hard drive partitions to optimize memory.

→ **Enable hardware to work:** Set up Small Computer System Interface (SCSI) devices and high-performance peripherals, such as scanners and CD recorders.

Get ready to . . .

Install a Printer

1. Read the instructions that came with the printer. Some printers require that you install software before connecting them, but others can be connected right away.

2. Turn on your computer and then follow the option that fits your needs:

    *   If your printer is a Plug-and-Play device, connect it, and Windows installs what it needs automatically.

    *   Insert the disc that came with the device and follow the on-screen instructions.

    *   Choose Start⇨Control Panel⇨Printers and Faxes⇨ Add A Printer. If this is the option that you're following, proceed to the next step in this list.

3. If you choose the third option in Step 2, in the Add Printer Wizard, click the Local Printer option (see Figure 7-1). Make sure that the Automatically Detect and Install My Plug and Play Printer check box is selected, and then click Next.

4. In the resulting Local or Network Printer dialog box, you see that Windows can't detect any printers. (This is likely, because if Windows could have, it should have done so automatically, but it doesn't hurt to try, does it?) Click Next.

5. In the resulting Select a Printer Port screen (see Figure 7-2), scroll the port list and select another option if you don't want to use the default LPT1 port. (A printer port is essentially where you plug the printer into your computer.) LPT2 and LPT3 are other printer port options, or you might be using a USB or network port that should appear in this list. Select the printer port and click Next.

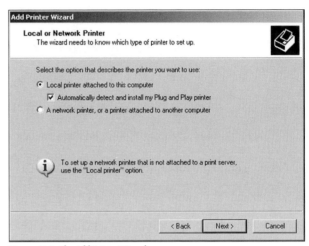

Figure 7-1: The Add Printer Wizard

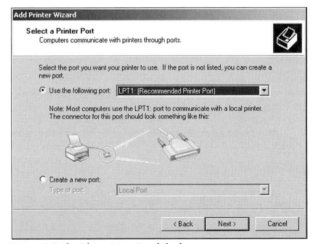

Figure 7-2: The Select a Printer Port dialog box

6. In the resulting Install Printer Software dialog box (see Figure 7-3), select a Manufacturer and then select a Printer. You then have two options:

   • If you have the manufacturer's disc, insert it in the appropriate CD drive now and click the Have Disk button. Click Next.

   • If you don't have the manufacturer's disc, click the Windows Update button to see a list of printer drivers that you can download from Microsoft's Web site. Click Next.

7. In the resulting Name Your Printer dialog box, enter a printer name and select Yes or No to determine whether you want this as your *default printer* (the one that Windows uses automatically for print jobs). Click Next.

8. In the resulting Print Test Page dialog box, leave the default option of Yes selected. Click Next to print a test page. Click Finish in the Completing the Add Printer Wizard window to complete the Add Printer Wizard.

9. Go to the Control Panel and choose Printers and Faxes, and then click the View Installed Printers or Fax Printers link. In the printer list, the default printer has a check mark next to it in the Printers and Faxes window shown in Figure 7-4.

You can use the Printer Tasks listed on the left of the window shown in Figure 7-4 to control printing or to change printer preferences.

If your computer is on a network, you get an additional dialog box in the wizard right after you name the printer. Select the Do Not Share This Printer option to stop others from using the printer, or you can select the Share Name option and enter a printer name to share the printer on your network. This means that others can see and select this printer to print to.

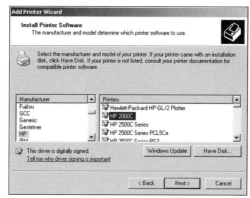

Figure 7-3: The Install Printer Software dialog box

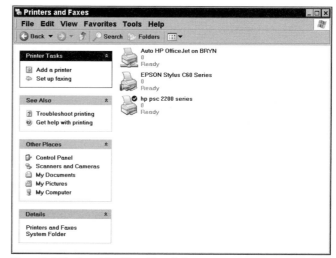

Figure 7-4: The Control Panel lists all installed printers

Set a Default Printer

1. Choose Start⇨Control Panel⇨Printers and Faxes⇨View Installed Printers or Fax Printers.

2. In the resulting Printers and Faxes window (shown in Figure 7-5), the current default printer is indicated by a check mark next to it.

3. Right-click any printer that isn't set as the default and choose Set as Default Printer from the shortcut menu, as shown in Figure 7-6.

4. Click the Close button in the Printers and Faxes window to save the new settings.

 To modify printing properties (for example, whether the printer prints in draft or high quality mode or uses color or only black and white), you can right-click a printer in the dialog box, shown previously in Figure 7-4, and choose Printing Preferences. This same dialog box is available from most common Windows-based software programs, such as Microsoft Word or Excel, by clicking the Properties button in the Print dialog box.

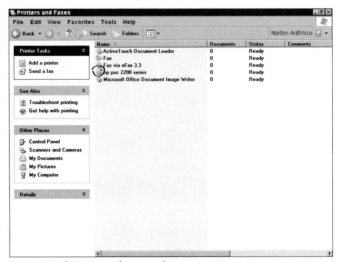

Figure 7-5: The Printers and Faxes window

Figure 7-6: The shortcut menu

Configure a USB Device

1. Choose Start⇨Control Panel⇨System.

2. In the resulting System Properties dialog box, click the Hardware tab and then click the Device Manager button.

3. In the resulting Device Manager dialog box, click the plus sign to the left of the Universal Serial Bus Controllers item. Right-click an item and choose Properties.

4. In the resulting Properties dialog box, click the General tab, shown in Figure 7-7. Here you can disable or enable the device by clicking the arrow on the Device Usage drop-down list box and selecting the Use This Device option or the Do Not Use This Device option.

5. Click the Driver tab, shown in Figure 7-8. Click the buttons on the Driver sheet to manage the driver; you can view details about it, upgrade it to a newer version, or uninstall it.

6. Click OK to save your USB device settings.

 If a USB device isn't working properly, click the Troubleshoot button on the General tab of the USB Device Properties dialog box. This opens the Windows Help and Support Center, with the USB Troubleshooter displayed. This takes you through a series of questions that help you test the device and narrow down the problem, and then provides suggestions for solving it.

Figure 7-7: The General tab

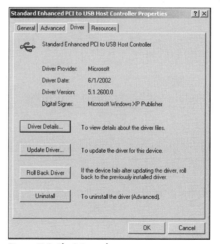

Figure 7-8: The Driver tab

Set Up a Modem

1. Choose Start⇨Control Panel⇨System.

2. In the resulting System Properties dialog box, click the Hardware tab and then the Device Manager button.

3. In the resulting Device Manager window, click the plus sign to the left of the Modems to display installed modem devices (see Figure 7-9). Right-click a modem and choose Properties.

4. In the resulting Properties dialog box, click the Modem tab, shown in Figure 7-10. You can adjust the following settings on this tab sheet:

   - **Speaker volume:** Turn the speaker on or off by using the Speaker Volume slider to determine whether you hear a dialing sound when the modem operates.

   - **Maximum Port Speed:** Adjust this setting by selecting a speed from the drop-down list. This setting determines the speed at which programs can send data to the modem. Although this is usually set at the correct number when you install the modem, if you're using a device that can support higher speeds (a Windows CE device is one example), you might want to manually change this to a higher setting.

   - **Dial Control:** Make sure that this check box is selected and click the Driver tab.

5. On the resulting Driver tab sheet, click the buttons on the Driver sheet to manage the driver; you can view details about it, upgrade it to a newer version, or uninstall it.

6. Click OK to save your settings.

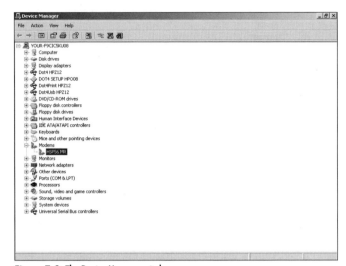

Figure 7-9: The Device Manager window

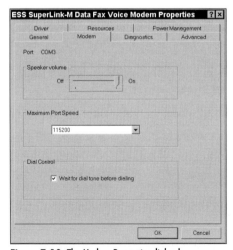

Figure 7-10: The Modem Properties dialog box

Set Up a New Monitor

1. Place the CD that came with your monitor in your CD-ROM drive and choose Start⇨Control Panel⇨System.

2. In the System Properties dialog box, click the Hardware tab and then the Device Manager button.

3. In the resulting Device Manager window, click the plus sign to the left of Monitors to display installed monitors (see Figure 7-11). Right-click the new monitor and choose Scan for Hardware Changes from the menu that appears.

4. In the resulting Hardware Update Wizard (see Figure 7-12), follow the wizard screens to install the monitor drivers.

5. When the wizard is complete, if everything seems to be working fine, you can close the Device Manager window.

 If you're having problems with the monitor, in the Device Manager window, right-click the monitor and choose Properties. In the resulting Monitor Properties dialog box in the Device Usage drop-down list, make sure that the Use this Device (Enable) option is selected. If things still aren't working right, click the Troubleshoot button and follow the on-screen directions.

 Many manufacturers' device drivers are already stored in Windows. When you install a device by using the Hardware Update Wizard, you might find that you can simply browse the manufacturers' device drivers rather than download them or select them from a CD.

 You can make adjustments to your monitor display by using the Appearance or Themes tabs of the Display Properties dialog box or the Display item in Windows Classic view of Control Panel options. For more about making Display option settings, take a gander at Chapter 10.

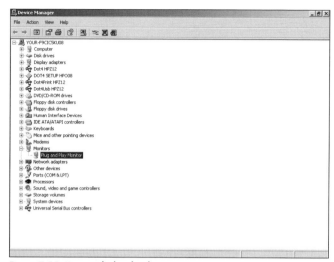

Figure 7-11: Monitors displayed in the Device Manager

Figure 7-12: A Hardware Update Wizard screen

Upgrade a Graphics Card

1. Turn off your computer. (*Note:* This step is very important; you have to open up your CPU for this procedure, and you're in danger of severe electrical shock if you leave your computer on while you play around inside it.)

2. Refer to your computer manual to determine how to open the CPU, how your computer is configured, where graphics cards can be interested, and which kinds of graphics cards to use.

3. Plug the graphics card into the appropriate slot, close your computer, and replace any screws that you took out when opening the computer up.

4. Turn on the computer; Windows detects the new card and installs appropriate drivers.

5. View the information about the installed graphics device by choosing Start➪Control Panel➪System. Click the Hardware tab of the System Properties dialog box that appears, and then click Device Manager.

6. Click the plus sign next to Display Adapters (see Figure 7-13), right-click the graphics card you installed, and choose Properties from the menu that appears. You see system settings for this card, and you can click the Troubleshoot button to troubleshoot through the Help and Support Center (see Figure 7-14) or get updated device drivers.

 Note that your particular hardware might have its own idiosyncrasies, and new technologies come along that change the way newer computers are configured, so be sure to read your computer users' manual before dealing with any hardware upgrade.

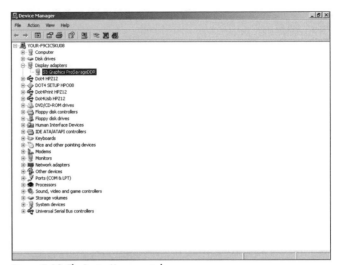

Figure 7-13: The Device Manager window

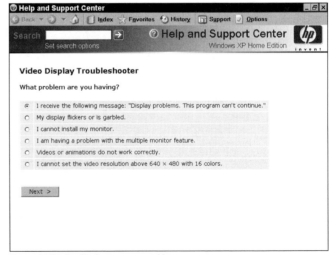

Figure 7-14: Troubleshooting your problems away

Set Up a Sound Card

1. Choose Start➪Control Panel➪Sounds and Audio Devices.

2. In the Sounds and Audio Devices dialog box, which opens with the Volume tab sheet displayed, click the Hardware tab to modify sound devices.

3. Click the sound card that you want to modify, as shown in Figure 7-15, and then click the Properties button.

4. In the resulting Audio Device Properties dialog box, click the arrow on the Device Usage drop-down list and select the Use This Device (Enable) setting if it isn't already selected.

5. If you want to make changes to the driver, click the Driver tab (see Figure 7-16), and then click the Update Driver button.

6. When you're done making settings, click OK.

 Read your users' manual before doing this procedure. Some sound cards are built into the motherboard, but others require that you take some steps to disable the old card before installing the new.

 The Sound Troubleshooter, which you can access from the Hardware sheet of the Sound and Audio Device Properties dialog box, takes you through testing your sound card step by step and isolating various problems. But remember the basics: You have to have speakers connected to your computer, and the volume setting on your computer can't be muted. If you neglect to properly set either of these two vital requirements, don't be ashamed — just about everyone has done it, myself included!

Figure 7-15: The Sounds and Audio Devices dialog box, Hardware tab

Figure 7-16: The Audio Device Properties dialog box, Driver tab

Set Up a Hardware Profile

1. After you set up the various hardware configurations that you prefer to use (such as printer, sound card, and so on), choose Start⇨Control Panel⇨System.

2. In the resulting System Properties dialog box, click the Hardware tab, and then the Hardware Profiles button. The Hardware Profiles dialog box, shown in Figure 7-17, appears.

3. Click a hardware profile (usually Hardware 1), and then click Copy to create a new hardware profile.

4. In the resulting Copy Profile dialog box (see Figure 7-18), enter a name for the new profile and click OK. Now you can select this hardware profile and do several things:

   • Click Properties to set up properties for any hardware, such as a laptop computer with associated docking station, desktop computer, and so on.

   • Click Rename to rename the hardware profile.

   • Click Delete to delete it.

   • Move the hardware profile so that it's first on the list and select the Select First Profile Listed option to have Windows use it as the default hardware profile.

5. After you make your settings for the new profile, click OK twice.

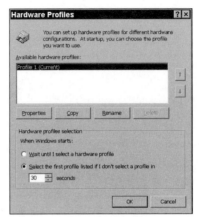

Figure 7-17: The Hardware Profiles dialog box

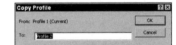

Figure 7-18: The Copy Profile dialog box

 A hardware profile essentially tells its buddy Windows which hardware to run and with what settings when Windows start up. When you install Windows, all installed devices are set up in Profile 1. The big benefit of using different hardware profiles comes with portable computers, which might use one set of hardware in your office, another set at home, and still another set on the road. So, create a hardware profile for each location and switch to it when you're on the move.

Use Disk Management to Create a Partition

1. Choose Start➪Control Panel➪Administrative Tools.

2. In the resulting Administrative Tools windows, double-click the Computer Management link.

3. In the resulting Computer Management window (shown in Figure 7-19), choose Disk Management in the left pane, right-click a basic disk in the right pane (this is usually your hard drive) that isn't allocated, and then choose New Partition.

4. Follow the steps in the New Partition Wizard to create the new partition.

 A new partition can free up some memory and make your system utilize memory more efficiently. But just so you know, you have to be logged on as a system administrator to complete the steps listed here.

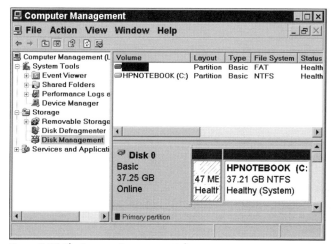

Figure 7-19: The Computer Management window

Maintaining and Protecting Windows

Chapter

8

This chapter is something like changing the oil in your car: It's not a barrel of laughs, but it keeps your car (or in this case, your computer) running, so it has to be done. These are the types of tasks that help you organize, maintain, and protect your computer system.

To keep your computer and Windows in tip-top shape, you need to organize files in logical ways, perform maintenance activities, prepare for disaster, and know how to recover from it.

The tasks in this chapter fall into three different categories:

➡ **Prevent and repair damage:** Some of these are fairly obvious, such as backing up files so that you have a copy in case of a crash. In addition, you can create a *system restore point,* which is essentially a copy of all your system settings; you can use system restore points to restore your computer to a happier, healthier state when it experiences problems. Finally, if you do have a serious disaster, you might need to start Windows in Safe Mode, which is a boot mode that loads only the most basic files and drivers.

➡ **Basic maintenance:** These tasks are the equivalent of a janitorial service. To keep your system in shape, you can *defragment,* or clean up, your hard drive. You can also delete cookies and temporary files. And you can schedule routine maintenance tasks to happen automatically so you don't take a chance that you forget to perform them.

➡ **Organizing things:** In this category is the task of creating a new user account. You would do this so that different people who access your computer can log on to their own accounts with their own settings.

Back Up Files to a CD-ROM or DVD-ROM

1. Place a CD or DVD in your CD-ROM or DVD-ROM drive, and then choose Start⇨My Documents.

2. In the resulting My Documents window (see Figure 8-1), select all the files that you want to copy to CD-ROM.

3. Right-click the files that you've selected and choose Send To⇨[Name of your CD-ROM or DVD-ROM drive].

4. To open your CD-ROM or DVD-ROM drive, click anywhere in the balloon that appears from the taskbar telling you that you have files to be written to the CD (see Figure 8-2).

5. Click the Write These Files to CD link. When the files have been copied, click the Close button to close the CD-ROM or DVD-ROM window.

 If you want to backup the entire contents of a folder, such as the My Document folder, you can just click the My Documents folder itself in Step 2.

 The balloon that appears when you've sent files to be written to a removable storage media is temporary, meaning that it could disappear before you've gotten around to clicking it. If so, just click the My Computer link in the Other Places section of the My Documents window, and then double-click the appropriate CD-ROM or DVD-ROM drive to open it. It appears just like the one in Figure 8-2, with the link to write the files available to you.

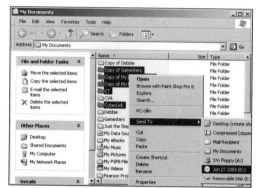

Figure 8-1: Files selected for backup in the My Documents window

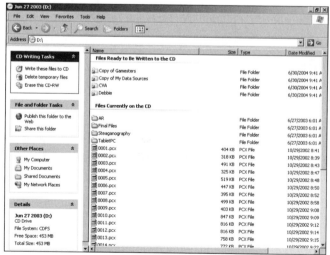

Figure 8-2: Files waiting to be copied to a CD

Create a System Restore Point

1. Choose Start⇨All Programs⇨Accessories⇨System
Tools⇨System Restore.

2. In the resulting dialog box, as shown in Figure 8-3,
select Create a Restore Point and then click Next.

3. In the resulting Create a Restore Point dialog box, enter
a name for the restore point (the current date and time
will be added to whatever you enter) and then click
Create.

4. In the resulting Restore Point Created dialog box, click
the Home button to return to the System Restore opening dialog box.

5. Select the Restore My Computer to an Earlier Time radio
button and then click Next. You see the restore point
that you created listed there, and you can select it and
proceed with the System Restore process.

If you haven't created a system restore point that is a logical place
to return to, and you experience problems, you can select a date
from the calendar in the window shown in Figure 8-4 and restore to
that date. If possible, pick one that would fall before any major
change that you might recently have made to your system, such as
installing a new piece of hardware or updating a driver.

Note that Windows Service Pack 2 includes alerts to attachments
spread through Internet Explorer, Outlook Express, and Windows
Messenger, which might help you protect your system from crashes
and other problems to save you from even having to do a System
Restore. See Chapter 12 for more about SP2.

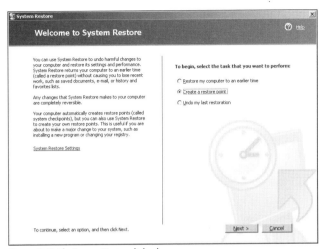
Figure 8-3: The System Restore dialog box

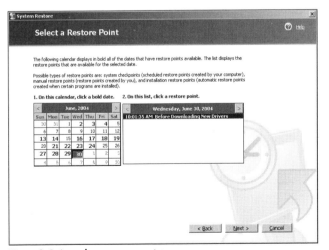
Figure 8-4: A saved system restore point

Defragment a Hard Drive

1. Choose Start⇨All Programs⇨Accessories⇨System Tools⇨Disk Defragmenter.

2. In the resulting Disk Defragmenter window, shown in Figure 8-5, select your hard drive (this usually is the C: drive).

3. To analyze your drive and see what defragmenting will do to it, click the Analyze button. After a few moments, a dialog box appears and suggests one of two courses of action:

   • No defragmentation is necessary. In this case, simply click OK and then close the Disk Defragmenter window.

   • Defragmentation is recommended. In this case, click Defragment. When the Defragmenter is done, close the Disk Defragmenter window.

You can also click the View Report button from this dialog box to view the details of the analysis, as shown in Figure 8-6.

Warning: Disk defragmenting could take a while. If you have energy-saving features such as screen saver active, they could cause the defragmenter to stop and start all over again. Try doing this overnight, while you're happily dreaming of much more interesting things.

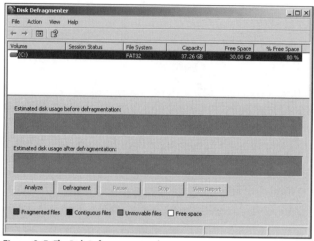

Figure 8-5: The Disk Defragmenter window

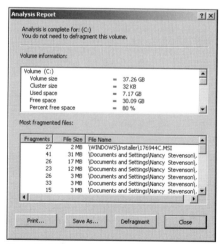

Figure 8-6: The results of a hard drive analysis

Clean Up a Drive

1. Choose Start⇨All Programs⇨Accessories⇨System Tools⇨Disk Cleanup, as shown in Figure 8-7.

2. If you have more than one hard drive, select the drive you want to clean up from the drop-down list and click OK.

3. The resulting dialog box tells you that Disk Cleanup is calculating how much space can be cleared on your hard drive. Go ahead and read your daily horoscope while it does its thing.

4. After a few moments, the Disk Cleanup For dialog box shown in Figure 8-8 appears. It displays the suggested files to delete in a list (those to be deleted have a check mark). If you want to select additional files in the list to delete, click to place a check mark next to them.

5. After you select all the files to delete, click OK. The selected files are deleted.

 Click the More Options tab in the Disk Cleanup dialog box to look at Windows components and program files that you don't use and system restore points that you might delete to save even more space.

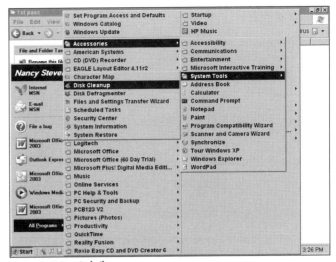

Figure 8-7: Start Disk Cleanup

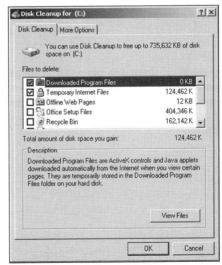

Figure 8-8: The Disk Cleanup dialog box

Delete Temporary Internet Files by Using Internet Explorer

1. Open Internet Explorer.

2. Choose Tools⇨Internet Options.

3. In the resulting Internet Options dialog box, on the General tab (see Figure 8-9) click the Delete Files button.

4. In the resulting dialog box, shown in Figure 8-10, if you want to delete offline files (copies of Web pages that you've chosen to view offline) select the Delete All Offline Content option.

5. Click OK and then close the Internet Options dialog box.

 Temporary Internet files can be deleted when you run Disk Cleanup (see that task earlier in this chapter), but the process that I describe here allows you to delete them without having to make choices about deleting other files on your system.

 You can also access the Internet Options dialog box from the Windows Control Panel. Choose Start⇨Control Panel, click Network and Internet Connections, and then click the Internet Options link.

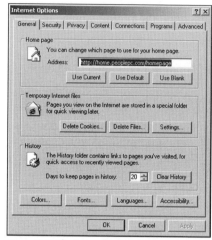

Figure 8-9: The Internet Options dialog box

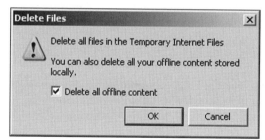

Figure 8-10: The Delete Files dialog box

Delete Cookies by Using Internet Explorer

1. Open Internet Explorer.

2. Choose Tools⇨Internet Options.

3. In the resulting Internet Options dialog box, on the General tab (see Figure 8-11) click the Delete Cookies button.

4. In the resulting dialog box, click OK to delete all cookies, as shown in Fiure 8-12, and then close the Internet Options dialog box.

 When you're in the Internet Options dialog box shown in Figure 8-11, if you want to remove all sites from the Internet Explorer History record, you can just click the Clear History button. This is useful if you've been shopping for birthday presents and don't want your significant other to know what you've been looking at.

 With Windows Service Pack 2 installed, enhanced security settings help you control what can and can't be downloaded to your computer from a central place called Security Center. Look at Chapter 12 for more about these features.

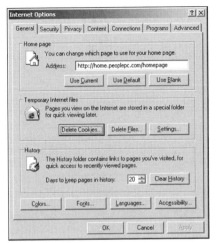

Figure 8-11: The Internet Options dialog box

Figure 8-12: The Scheduled Tasks dialog box

Schedule Maintenance Tasks

1. Choose Start⇨All Programs⇨Accessories⇨System Tools⇨Scheduled Tasks.

2. In the resulting dialog box, double-click the Add a Scheduled Task icon.

3. In the resulting Scheduled Task Wizard, click Next to proceed.

4. In the resulting dialog box, shown in Figure 8-13, select the program that you want to run (for example, Disk Cleanup or your antivirus program) and then click Next.

5. In the next dialog box (see Figure 8-14), select the frequency for running the program (Daily, Weekly, Monthly, One Time Only, When My Computer Starts, or When I Log On), and then click Next.

6. In the resulting dialog box, select a start time and start date by clicking the arrows in each field, and then click Next.

7. In the following dialog box, enter your user name and password for Windows XP. If your computer is password protected, some tasks might not run if you don't enter this information. Click Next.

8. On the resulting screen, the schedule task is confirmed; click Finish to complete the procedure.

 If you are set up to require a password to log onto Windows and you don't enter a password in Step 7, your task won't run.

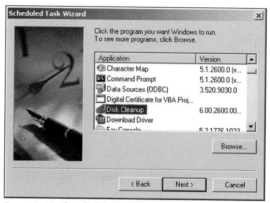

Figure 8-13: The Scheduled Task Wizard

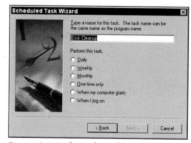

Figure 8-14: Choose how often to perform the task

 On the final wizard screen, you can select the Open Advanced Properties for This Task When I Click Finish check box to display a dialog box that offers settings that control things like whether the task should run if the computer is running off batteries and whether the task should be stopped if it takes more than a certain number of minutes to complete.

Create a New User Account

1. Choose Start⇨Control Panel.

2. In the resulting window, double-click the User Accounts link.

3. In the User Accounts window, click the Create a New Account link.

4. In the resulting dialog box, shown in Figure 8-15, enter a name for the account and click Next.

5. In the next dialog box, shown in Figure 8-16, select the type of account you want to create: a Computer Administrator who can do things like create and change accounts and install programs; or a Limited user who can't do those tasks. Click the Create Account button, and then close the Control Panel.

 After you create an account, you can make changes to it, such as assigning a password or changing the account type, by double-clicking it in the Control Panel, User Account window you reached in Step 3 of this task and following the links listed there.

Figure 8-15: Naming a new user account

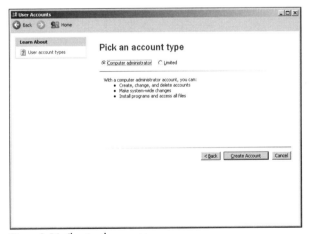

Figure 8-16: Choosing the account type

Part IV
Customizing Windows

Customizing the Windows Desktop

Chapter

9

You chose your designer day planner, glow in the dark gel pens, and solid maple inbox for your real world desktop, right? Why shouldn't the Windows desktop give you the same flexibility to make things look the way you like? After all, this is the main work area of Windows, a space that you traverse many, many times in a typical work day. Take it from somebody who spends many hours in front of a computer: Customizing the desktop pays off in increased productivity, as well as decreased eye strain.

To customize the desktop, you can do the following:

- **Change the way the desktop looks:** Set up Windows to display images and colors. You can also use screen saver settings to switch from everyday work stuff to a pretty animation when you've stopped working for a time.

- **Rearrange icons:** The desktop isn't just a pretty picture. Placed on the background are icons that represent shortcuts to the programs and files that you work with every day. Organizing these icons logically can help you be more efficient.

- **Connect your desktop to the online world:** Active Desktop, the feature of Windows that allows you to keep a live Internet site on your desktop, is a mixed blessing. It can keep you constantly in tune with what's going on in the world while slowing down your computer as it chomps up computer power like a person eating popcorn at a movie. Whether it's a feature you want to use or not, this chapter helps you set up Active Desktop to see whether it's a good fit for you.

Get ready to . . .

Set Your Screen's Resolution

1. Right-click the desktop to display a shortcut menu, and then choose Properties.

2. In the resulting Display Properties dialog box shown in Figure 9-1, click the Settings tab.

3. On the Settings tab, click the slider in the Screen Resolution area and move it to a higher or lower resolution.

 Higher resolutions, such as 1400 x 1050, produce smaller, crisper images. Lower resolutions, such as 800 x 600, produce larger, somewhat jagged images. The up side of higher resolution is that more fits on your screen; the down side is that words and graphics can be hard to see. One option: If fonts appear too small to read, change the Font Size setting on the Appearance tab of the Display Properties dialog box to be Large or Extra Large.

4. Click OK to accept the new screen resolution.

Change the Desktop Image

1. Right-click the desktop and choose Properties from the shortcut menu.

2. In the resulting Display Properties dialog box, click the Desktop tab to display it, as shown in Figure 9-2.

3. Select a desktop background option in the Background list box.

Figure 9-1: The Display Properties dialog box, Settings tab

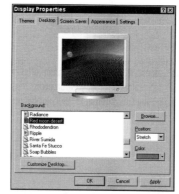

Figure 9-2: The Display Properties dialog box, Desktop tab

4. In the Position drop-down list, select one of the following options:

- **Center:** Quite logically, this option centers the image on a colored background so that you can see a border of color around its edges.

- **Tile:** Displays multiple copies of the image filling the desktop. The number of images depends on the size and resolution of the original graphic.

- **Stretch:** Stretches one copy of the image to fill the screen, covering any background color completely.

5. Click the arrow for the Color drop-down list to display a palette of colors. (This color is visible if you select the Center position setting.) Click a color in the palette or click the Other button to see a larger spectrum of colors to choose from.

6. You can click the Apply button to apply the settings and see what they look like, or just click OK to apply the settings and close the dialog box. Figure 9-3 shows the setting applied.

 If you don't want an image on your desktop, choose None for your background and then choose a color from the Color drop-down palette. If you don't like the colors offered, you can access a whole range of colors by clicking the Other button in the Color Palette.

Figure 9-3: Apply the Setting

 If you apply a desktop theme (see more about this in the following task), you overwrite whatever desktop settings you've made in this task, and if you apply a desktop theme and then go back and make desktop settings, you'll replace the theme's settings. But making changes is easy, and it keeps your desktop interesting, so play around with themes and desktop backgrounds all you like!

Use Your Own Image for the Desktop

1. Right-click the desktop and choose Properties from the shortcut menu.

2. In the Display Properties dialog box, click the Desktop tab to display it (see Figure 9-4), and then click the Browse button.

3. In the Browse dialog box, locate a graphics file on your hard drive or storage media (for example, a CD-ROM) and click Open to add that image to the list of backgrounds.

4. Click OK to select the background as your desktop background.

5. In the Position drop-down list, select one of the following options:

   • **Center:** Quite logically, this option centers the image on a colored background so that you can see a border of color around its edges.

   • **Tile:** Displays multiple copies of the image filling the desktop. The number of images depends on the size and resolution of the original graphic.

   • **Stretch:** Stretches one copy of the image to fill the screen, covering any background color completely.

6. Click the arrow on the Color field to display a palette of colors (this is the color that would be visible if you chose the Center position setting). Click a color in the palette, or click Other to see a larger spectrum of colors to choose from.

7. You can click the Apply button to apply the settings and see what they look like, or just click OK to apply the settings and close the dialog box. Figure 9-5 shows the settings applied.

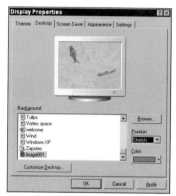

Figure 9-4: Select your own image

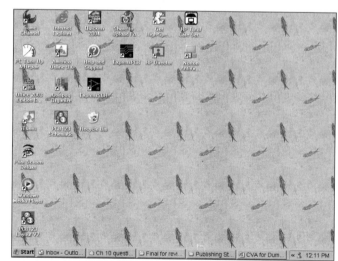

Figure 9-5: Apply the image

Choose a Desktop Theme

1. Right-click the desktop and choose Properties. The Display Properties dialog box opens. Click the Themes tab.

2. On the resulting Themes tab, shown in Figure 9-6, select a theme from the Theme drop-down list. Your options include the following:

   - **Windows XP** offers up a rolling meadow and clouds against a blue sky. The color scheme that this theme uses for various on-screen elements, such as window title bars, relies heavily on blues and reds.

   - **Windows Classic** sports a plain blue background with silvery-blue colors for screen elements.

   - **More Themes Online** is a link to a Microsoft Web page (see Figure 9-7) where you can buy Microsoft Plus!, a software collection of desktop themes. This will run you about $20.00. Several of the themes you can get with Microsoft Plus! are animated. These are cute, but be forewarned that they can take a chunk of your computer memory to run.

   - **Browse** takes you to the Program folder of Windows, where you can look for any files with the .Theme extension. It's not that Windows comes with a lot of these waiting in this folder for you to use them, but if you buy and install Microsoft Plus!, the new themes are stored here by default. If you find one you like, select and click the Open button.

3. Click OK to apply the selected theme.

 You can use the settings on the Appearance tab of the Display dialog box to modify the color scheme that comes preset with Themes. On the Advanced tab, you can specify colors, fonts, and font sizes element by element. (For example, choose one color for dialog box title bars, another for icons, menus, and so on.) If you go to the trouble of creating such a customized color scheme, consider saving it by displaying the Themes tab, clicking Save As, and giving a name to your new look.

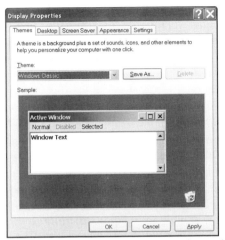

Figure 9-6: The Display Properties dialog box, Themes tab

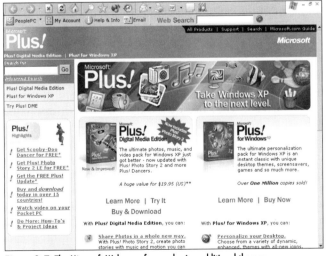

Figure 9-7: The Microsoft Web page for purchasing additional themes

Arrange Icons on the Desktop

1. Modify the icons displayed on your desktop by using any of these methods:

   - Right-click the Windows desktop and in the resulting shortcut menu, shown in Figure 9-8, choose Arrange Icons By, and then choose one of four criteria: Name, Size, Type, or Modified.

   - Click any icon on the desktop and drag it to a new location.

   - Right-click the Windows desktop and choose Arrange Icons By, and then make sure that Auto Arrange isn't selected. (If it is selected, deselect it.) Now you can click any icon and drag it to another location on the desktop.

2. To automatically add certain folders to your desktop, right-click the desktop and choose Properties. Click the Desktop tab, and then click the Customize Desktop button.

3. In the resulting Desktop Items dialog box, shown in Figure 9-9, select any of the Desktop Icons check boxes to automatically display a shortcut for Internet Explorer, the My Documents folder, My Computer, or My Network Places.

4. Click OK twice to save the settings.

 To change an icon used for the preset folders that you set up in the Desktop Items dialog box, click the Change Icon button in the Desktop Items dialog box. In the Change Icon dialog box that appears, click another icon, and then click OK twice. However, be careful when using this feature: If somebody who uses your computer isn't aware of the changed icons, he could start clicking the wrong icon and potentially not only waste time but run a program that you don't want him to run. If you make changes and decide to go back to Microsoft's original idea of a good icon for programs, click the Restore Default button in the Desktop Items dialog box.

Figure 9-8: The shortcut menu

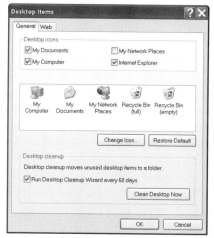

Figure 9-9: The Desktop Items dialog box

Enable Active Desktop

1. Right-click the desktop and choose Properties. Click the Desktop tab, and then click the Customize Desktop button.

2. In the resulting Desktop Items dialog box, click the Web tab to display it, as shown in Figure 9-10. In the Web Pages area, select the My Current Home Page item.

3. Alternatively, you can click the New button to select another Web page to display on your desktop. The New Desktop Item dialog box appears, as shown in Figure 9-11, offering the following options:

   - Click the Visit Gallery button to open a Microsoft Internet Explorer Desktop Gallery site. Here you find an Investor Ticker, CBS SportsLine, Weather Map from MSNBC, and more. Just click the Add to Active Desktop button to add each item.

   - Enter the URL of a Web page that you'd like to display on your desktop in the Location text box.

   - Click the Browse button to locate an HTML document or picture to place on your desktop. This opens your Internet Explorer Favorites folder, where you can select a favorite site and click Open to specify it.

4. To save your new Active Desktop settings, click OK.

 With several types of online connections, such as cable, providing an always-on connection mode, you might find that rather than using Active Desktop, you can just as easily keep your browser open to the page that you want to view and choose View⟹Refresh every now and then. This diverts less of your computer's resources to keeping online information constantly refreshed.

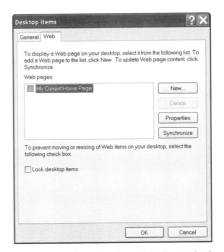

Figure 9-10: The Desktop Items dialog box, Web tab

Figure 9-11: The New Desktop Item dialog box

Set Up a Screen Saver

1. Right-click the desktop and choose Properties. Click the Screen Saver tab to display it, as shown in Figure 9-12.

2. In the Screen Saver drop-down list, select a screen saver.

3. Use the arrows in the Wait text box to set the number of inactivate minutes that the Windows waits before displaying the screen saver.

4. Click the Preview button to take a peek at your screen saver of choice (see Figure 9-13). When you're happy with your settings, click OK.

 Screen savers used to be required to keep your monitor from burning out because one image was held on your screen for too long. Newer monitors don't require this, but people are attached to their screen savers, so the feature persists. Screen savers are also useful for hiding what's on your screen from a curious passersby if you happen to wander away from your desk for a while. If you want a more personalized screen saver experience than the rotating Windows logos provide, choose the My Pictures Slideshow from the list of screen savers. This displays the images saved in your My Pictures folder, one after another. Just make sure that you don't have anything in that folder that you'd rather keep private!

 Some screen savers allow you to modify their settings; for example, how fast they display or how many lines they draw on screen. To customize this when in the Display Properties dialog box on the Screen Saver tab, click the Settings button.

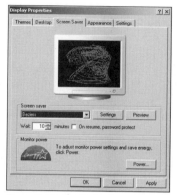

Figure 9-12: The Display Properties dialog box, Screen Saver tab

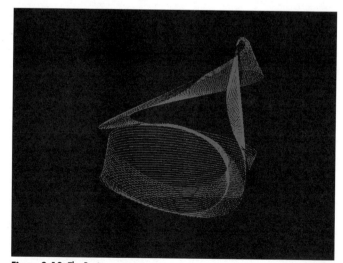

Figure 9-13: The Bezier screen saver

Change the Windows Color Scheme

1. Right-click the desktop and choose Properties.

2. In the resulting Display Properties dialog box, click the Appearance tab display it, as shown in Figure 9-14.

3. Select a color scheme from the Color Scheme drop-down list.

4. To customize the selected preset color scheme, click the Advanced button.

5. In the resulting Advanced Appearance dialog box, shown in Figure 9-15, select items one by one from the Item drop-down list. Make your changes by using the Size, Color, and Font settings.

6. Click OK to accept the advanced settings, and then click OK to close the Display Properties dialog box and apply all changes.

 When customizing a color scheme, be aware that not all screen elements allow you to modify all settings. For example, setting an Application Background doesn't make the Font setting available, because it's just a background setting. Makes sense, huh?

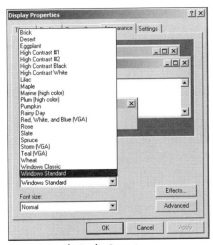

Figure 9-14: The Display Properties dialog box, Appearance tab

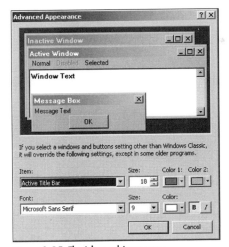

Figure 9-15: The Advanced Appearance dialog box

Customizing Windows Behavior

*P*eople aren't born with good manners. Everyone has to be taught to help other people and share toys, for example. Similarly, sometimes Windows has to be taught how to behave. For example, it doesn't know right off the bat that somebody using it has a vision challenge that requires special help, or that a user prefers a certain mouse cursor, or that you want to see file extensions when lists of files are displayed.

Somebody taught you manners, but Windows depends on you to make settings that customize its behavior. This is good news for you because the ability to customize Windows gives you a lot of flexibility in how you interact with it.

Here's what you can do to customize Windows:

➥ Control features that help visually challenged users to use a computer.

➥ Choose how folders and their contents are displayed, with choices ranging from thumbnail pictures of the contents to text listings.

➥ Set up the file type that an application is associated with to make opening and saving files simpler. Changing this involves associating file extensions (for example, .doc for Word documents and .xls for Excel files) with an application.

➥ Modify the mouse functionality for left-handed use, change the cursor to sport a certain look, or make the cursor easier to view as it moves around your screen.

Use Magnifier to Adjust Text Size

1. Choose Start⇨All Programs⇨Accessories⇨Accessibility⇨ Magnifier.

2. In the resulting dialog box, Click OK to move on.

3. In the resulting Magnifier Settings dialog box, adjust the settings to your liking:

   - **Magnification Level:** This controls how big things get on your screen.

   - **Tracking:** These settings control what is tracked on-screen, such as your mouse cursor, or where your insertion point is for text editing.

   - **Presentation:** Here's where you make settings that affect inverted colors (so your background is black and the text white), and how and when Magnifier is displayed.

4. Click the Minimize button on the Magnifier Settings dialog box to hide it. (Don't click Exit, or Magnifier turns off.)

5. In the Magnifier window, shown at the top of Figure 10-1, start working on your computer and you'll notice that, if you have the Follow Mouse Cursor option selected in the Magnifier Settings dialog box, you have two cursors on-screen. One cursor appears in the Magnifier window, and one appears in whatever is showing on your computer (for example, your desktop or an open application).

6. Maneuver either cursor to work in your document. (They're both active, so it does take some getting used to.)

7. When you want to close the Magnifier window, display the Magnifier Settings dialog box, shown in Figure 10-2, by clicking it on the taskbar, and click the Exit or the Close button.

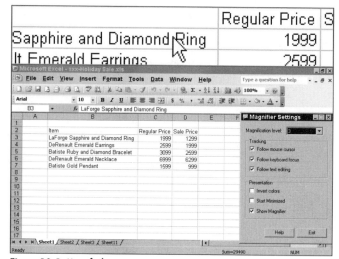

Figure 10-1: Magnified text

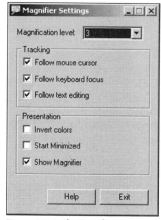

Figure 10-2: The Magnifier Settings dialog box

Set Up Narrator Text to Voice Options

1. Choose Start⇨All Programs⇨Accessories⇨Accessibility⇨ Narrator.

2. A dialog box appears, explaining the function and limitations of Narrator. Click OK to close it.

3. In the resulting Narrator dialog box, select any of the following check boxes (as shown in Figure 10-3):

   - Announce events on screen

   - Read typed characters

   - Move mouse pointer to active item

   - Start Narrator minimized

4. To control the characteristics of the Narrator voice, click the Voice button.

5. In the resulting Voice Settings dialog box (see Figure 10-4), select the narrator that you want to hear (only one is there by default, Microsoft Sam) and the Speed, Volume, and Pitch of the voice. Click OK to save Voice settings.

6. Click the Minimize button on the Narrator dialog box to hide it, and then begin working on your computer. (*Note:* Narrator can read only in English!)

7. When you finish, display the Narrator dialog box and click the Exit or the Close button.

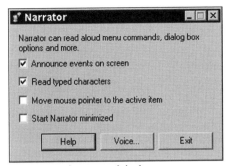

Figure 10-3: The Narrator dialog box

 By using settings in the Narrator dialog box, you can have Narrator narrate on-screen events or read the text you type. You can also make a setting to have the mouse cursor move to the place on-screen where an action is occurring.

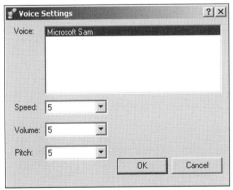

Figure 10-4: The Voice Settings dialog box

Use the On-Screen Keyboard Feature

1. Choose Start⇨All Programs⇨Accessories⇨Accessibility⇨ On-Screen Keyboard.

2. In the resulting keyboard (see Figure 10-5) and dialog box, click OK.

3. Open a document in any application where you can enter text, and then click the keys on the on-screen keyboard to make entries.

 To use keystroke combinations (such as Ctrl+Z), click first key (in this case, Ctrl), and then the second key (Z). You don't have to hold down the first key as you do with a regular keyboard.

4. To change settings, such as how you select keys (typing mode) or the font used to label keys (Font), choose Settings and then choose one of the four options shown in Figure 10-6.

5. Click the Close button to stop using the on-screen keyboard.

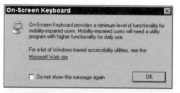

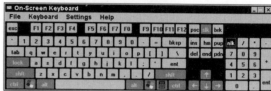

Figure 10-5: The On-Screen Keyboard

 You can set up the Hover typing mode to activate a key after you hover your mouse over it for a predefined period of time (*x* number of seconds). If you have arthritis or some other condition that makes clicking your mouse difficult, this option can help you enter text in documents. Choose Settings⇨Typing Mode⇨Hover to Select to activate the Hover mode.

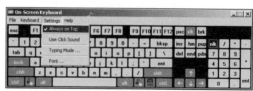

Figure 10-6: The Settings menu

Change Folder Options

1. Open any window where you view folders (for example, choose Start⇨My Documents).

2. Choose Tools⇨Folder Options.

3. In the resulting Folder Options dialog box (see Figure 10-7), make sure that the General tab is selected. Here you can adjust three kinds of settings:

   • To display folder management tasks on the left side of the window, as shown in Figure 10-8, select the Show Common Tasks in Folders option in the Tasks area.

   • To open folders in the same window or open a new window for every folder you open, use the Browse Folders settings.

   • To control whether you open items with a single or double-click, change the Click Items as Follows settings.

4. To save the new settings, click OK.

 One setting on the View tab of the Folder Options dialog box is worth pointing out: the Folder Views default. Folder views might always come up with the thumbnail view of files even though you might prefer the Detail view (the one that shows files in a list with the file type and date last modified) or another view. To reset the default view, just choose that view by clicking the Views button (located on the Standard toolbar in any folder window) and clicking the view that you prefer, and then open the Folder Options dialog box, click the View tab, and click the Apply to All Folders button. Now whenever you open a folder view, folders and files are displayed in your preferred format.

Figure 10-7: The Folder Options dialog box

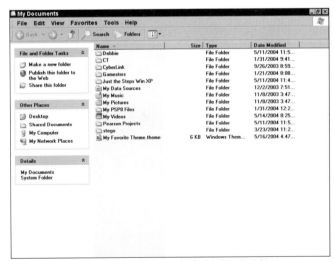

Figure 10-8: Folder management features (displayed along the left)

View File Extensions

1. Open any window where you view folders (for example, choose Start⇨My Documents).

2. Choose Tools⇨Folder Options.

3. In the resulting Folder Options dialog box, click the View tab to select it (see Figure 10-9).

4. In the Advanced Settings list, scroll down to locate the Hide Extensions for Known File Types check box and deselect it.

5. Click OK to apply the change and close the dialog box. Now file extensions appear in the folder view, as shown in Figure 10-10.

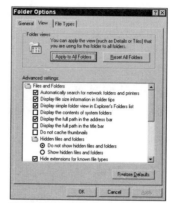

Figure 10-9: Folder Options dialog box

 Note that you can change the informational columns displayed in the Details view of files and folders (like the one shown in Figure 10-10) by right-clicking any of the column headings (such as Name or Size) and choosing other items from the shortcut menu, such as the date created or the name of the file or folder owner. You can even display details specifically for audio files, such as artist name and album title.

 A quick way to recognize compressed file types is to select Show Encrypted or Compressed NTFS Files in Color in the Advanced Settings list mentioned in Step 4.

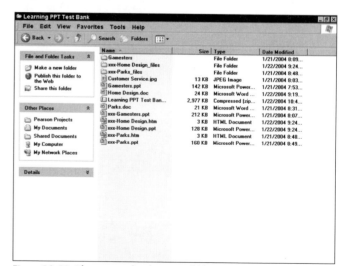

Figure 10-10: File extensions listed in a view folder

Associate a File Type with an Application

1. Open any window where you view folders (for example, choose Start⇨My Computer).

2. Choose Tools⇨Folder Options. The Folder Options dialog box appears. Click the File Types tab to select it (see Figure 10-11). Here you can make a few settings:

    *   To change the program that's used to open a certain file type (for example, if a .gif image file is opened by Microsoft Windows Picture and Fax Viewer, and you prefer to open it in Paint when you double-click it) click the file type in the Registered File Types list. Then, click the Change button. The Open With dialog box appears, as shown in Figure 10-12. Select a program name, and then click OK.

    *   To register a new file extension so that you can then associate a program with it, click the New button. The Create New Extension dialog box appears. Enter the extension in the File Extension text box, and then click the Advanced button. Select a file type from the Associated File Type drop-down to display that list. Click OK, and click OK again to save your settings and close the Folder Options dialog box.

Figure 10-11: The Folder Options dialog box, File Types tab

Figure 10-12: The Open With dialog box

Change the Cursor

1. Choose Start⇨Control Panel and double-click the Mouse link.

2. Click the Pointers tab in the Mouse Properties dialog box, shown in Figure 10-13. Whatever theme you have displayed in Windows is the one that will be selected here with its cursors displayed. To change to cursors used in other themes, select a theme from the Scheme drop-down list.

3. Click the Normal Select (or any other) cursor in the Customize list, and then click the Browse button.

4. In the resulting Browse dialog box, shown in Figure 10-14, click the Views button and choose Thumbnails.

5. Click a cursor file icon and then click Open.

6. Click Apply to see whether you're happy with your cursor choice, and when you are, click OK to exit.

 Be careful not to change the cursor to another standard cursor (for example, changing the Normal Select cursor to the Busy hourglass cursor). This could prove slightly confusing for you and completely baffling to anybody else who works on your computer. If you make a choice and decide it was a mistake, click the Use Default button on the Pointers tab in the Mouse Properties dialog box to return a selected cursor to its default choice.

Figure 10-13: The Mouse Properties dialog box, Pointers tab

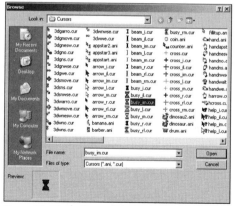

Figure 10-14: The Browse dialog box

Change Mouse Behavior

1. Choose Start⇨Control Panel and in the Pick a Category list, click the Printers and Other Hardware link.

2. In the resulting window (see Figure 10-15), in the Pick a Control Panel area, double-click the Mouse link.

3. In the resulting Mouse Properties dialog box, shown in Figure 10-16, select the Switch Primary and Secondary Buttons check box.

 You can use the Switch Primary and Secondary Buttons feature to make the right mouse button handle all the usual left button functions, such as clicking and dragging, and the left button handle the typical right-hand functions, such as displaying shortcut menus. This helps left-handed people use the mouse more easily.

4. Click OK to save the new setting.

 If you're experiencing any kind of repetitive stress symptoms due to conditions such as carpal tunnel syndrome, consider occasionally switching the mouse button functionality and using your other hand to operate the mouse. Many people find that they can get used to using either hand for mouse functions, and the temporary change might help delay or prevent serious damage to your hands or wrists.

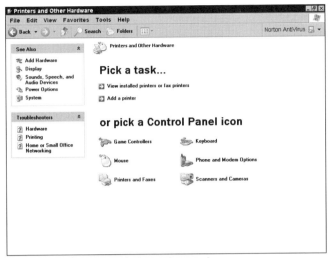

Figure 10-15: The Printers and Other Hardware window

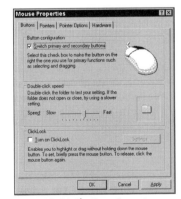

Figure 10-16: The Mouse Properties dialog box

Making Windows Secure

After working with Windows and the software that it supports for a while, you'll find that you've built up a treasure trove of information and documents. Microsoft provided security features in Windows that help to keep your information private, whether at work or home, and keep you in safe territory when you're online. You can do the following:

➡ **Use password protection:** Keep people from accessing your computer when you're not around. A Windows password stops people from logging on to Windows at all, and a screen saver password ensures that nobody can stop the screen saver from running without entering a password.

➡ **Share information:** Share folders with others on a network or to keep others out of folders, if you prefer. You can also use the shared folders feature to share folders with multiple users of a standalone computer.

➡ **Protect individual files:** Make them read only — that is, allowing people to read what's in them but not make and save changes — or hidden from others entirely.

➡ **Set up Internet Explorer zones:** Designate Trusted Web sites (from which you feel perfectly safe downloading files) and Restricted sites (which are likely to contain things that you wouldn't download to your worst enemy's computer).

Chapter

11

Get ready to . . .

Add or Change the Windows Password

1. Choose Start➪Control Panel, and double-click User Accounts.

2. In the User Accounts window, click the Change an Account link, and then on the next screen click an account to add the password to. Click the Create a Password link.

3. In the Create a Password for Your Account screen, shown in Figure 11-1, enter a password, confirm it, and add a password hint.

4. Click the Create Password button.

5. You're returned to the User Accounts window and the What Do You Want to Change about Your Account screen (see Figure 11-2), where you can click the Change My Password link, enter your old password, and then follow the procedure in Step 3 to change your password.

6. Click the Close button to close the User Accounts window.

 If you forget your password, Windows shows the hint you entered to help you remember it, but keep in mind that anybody who is using your computer can see the hint when it's displayed. So, if lots of people know that you drive a Ford, and your hint is "My car model," your password protection is about as effective as a thin raincoat in a hurricane.

 After you create a password, you can go to the User Accounts window and remove the password (by clicking the Remove My Password link).

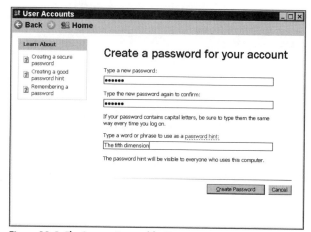

Figure 11-1: The Create a Password for Your Account screen

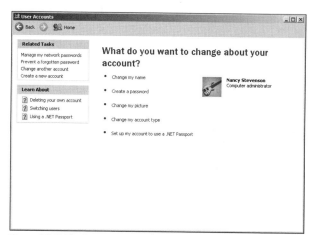

Figure 11-2: The User Accounts window

Use a Password-Protected Screen Saver

1. Choose Start⇨Control Panel, double-click Display (see Figure 11-3), and select the Screen Saver tab.

2. In the resulting Display Properties dialog box, select the On Resume, Password Protect check box (see Figure 11-4), and then click OK. If you're set up with multiple users, the selection here is On Resume, Display Welcome Screen.

3. When the screen saver activates, press a key or move your mouse to open the Display dialog box.

4. Enter your password (the one that you set up for Windows in the previous task) and click OK.

 You can change settings for your screen saver by clicking the Settings button on the Screen Saver tab of the Display Properties dialog box. In the resulting dialog box, you can modify the style of the screen saver objects, the color scheme, and the size and resolution of the image.

 If you don't have a Windows password set and you activate the screen saver password feature, just click OK when you see the Display dialog box mentioned in Step 3. The screen saver password feature requires a password only if one is set up for Windows. Otherwise, the Display dialog box is all show!

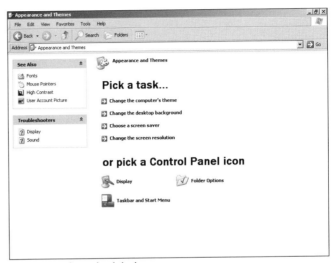

Figure 11-3: The Display dialog box

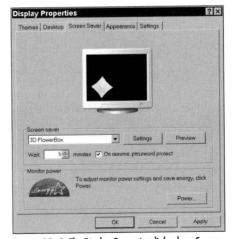

Figure 11-4: The Display Properties dialog box, Screen Saver tab

Use Shared Folders

1. Locate the folder that you want to share by using Windows Explorer. (Choose Start⇨All Programs⇨ Accessories⇨Windows Explorer.)

2. Right-click the folder that you want to share and choose Sharing and Security (see Figure 11-5).

3. In the resulting Properties dialog box, shown in Figure 11-6, select the Share this Folder on the Network check box if it's not already selected.

4. Enter a name for the folder to be visible to others in the Share Name text box.

5. Select the Allow Network Users to Change My Files check box to enable others to make changes, and click OK.

 To find out more about using Windows Explorer to locate and work with files, see Chapter 2.

 You can also use settings on the Sharing tab to make a folder private on a standalone computer by selecting the Make this Folder Private check box. When you do, anyone logged on to your computer as another user can't access the folder.

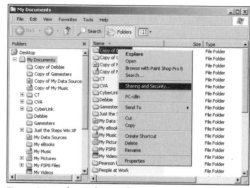

Figure 11-5: The Windows Explorer window

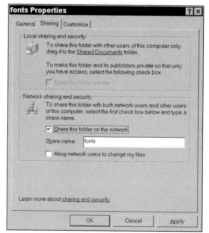

Figure 11-6: The Properties dialog box, Sharing tab

Set Up Trusted and Restricted Web Sites

1. Double-click the Internet Explorer icon on the Windows desktop to start the browser.

2. Choose Tools⇨Internet Options.

3. In the Internet Options dialog box (see Figure 11-7), click the Security tab.

4. Click the Trusted Sites or Restricted Sites icon and then click the Sites button.

5. In the resulting Trusted Sites dialog box, enter a URL for a trusted Web site in the Add This Web Site to the Zone text box.

6. Click Add to add the site to the list of Web sites, as shown in Figure 11-8.

7. Repeat Steps 3 through 6 to add more sites.

8. When you're done, click OK twice to close the dialog boxes.

You can establish a Privacy setting on the Privacy tab of the Internet Options dialog box to control which sites are allowed to download *cookies* to your computer. Cookies are tiny files that a site uses to track your online activity and recognize you when you return to the source site. Trusted sites are ones that you allow to download cookies to your computer even though the privacy setting you have made might not allow many other sites to do so. Restricted sites can never download cookies to your computer, no matter what your privacy setting is.

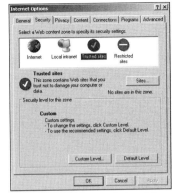

Figure 11-7: The Internet Options dialog box, Security tab

Note: If the Require Server Verification (https:) for All Sites In This Zone check box is selected in the Trusted Sites dialog box, any Trusted site you add must use the `https://` prefix, which indicates the site has a secure connection.

Figure 11-8: The Trusted Sites dialog box

Enable Internet Connection Firewall

1. Choose Start⇨My Network Places.

2. In the Network Places window, click the View Network Connections link.

3. In the resulting Network Connections window (see Figure 11-9), click the connection that you want to protect (in the right pane), and then click the Change Settings of This Connection link (in the left pane).

4. In the resulting Connection Properties dialog box, display the Advanced tab (see Figure 11-10).

5. Select the check box labeled Protect My Computer and Network by Limiting or Preventing Access to This Computer from the Internet, and then click OK.

 A *firewall* is a program that protects your computer from the outside world. This is generally a good thing, unless you use a Virtual Private Network (VPN). Using a firewall with a VPN results in you being unable to share files and use some other VPN features.

 If you install Windows Service Pack 2, firewall settings will work differently. The feature isn't even called Internet Connection Firewall, but is now Windows Firewall. See Chapter 12 to set up your firewall if you've installed SP2.

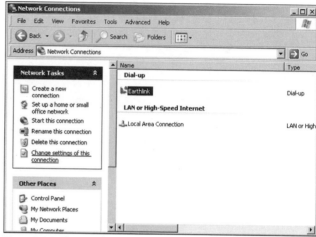

Figure 11-9: The Network Connections window

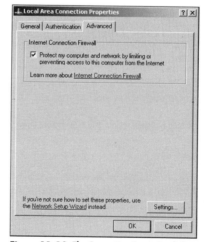

Figure 11-10: The Connection Properties dialog box, Advanced tab

Install a Security Patch by Using Windows Update

1. Choose Start⇨All Programs⇨Windows Update.

2. In the Windows Update window, shown in Figure 11-11, click the Scan for Updates link. Windows thinks about this for a while, so feel free to page through a magazine for a minute or two.

3. In the resulting window, click the Review and Install Updates link.

4. In the following window, which shows the available updates (see Figure 11-12), you can remove updates that you don't want to install. (So, if you want to install only the security updates, remove everything else by clicking the Remove button next to those items.)

5. Click the Install Now button to install selected updates. The Windows Update Web Page dialog box appears, showing the installation progress.

6. When the installation is complete, you might get a message telling you that it's a good idea to restart your computer to complete the installation. Click OK.

 I recommend creating a system restore point just before downloading updates. Some updates can cause problems, and being able to restore your system back to the moment before their installation could save you heartache. See Chapter 8 for more about creating a system restore point.

 Service Pack 2 provides more automated Windows Update features; if you use a dial up connection, SP2 also helps you download updates more easily. See Chapter 12 for more about these features.

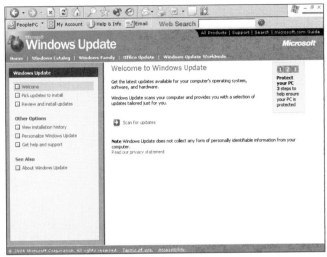

Figure 11-11: The Windows Update window

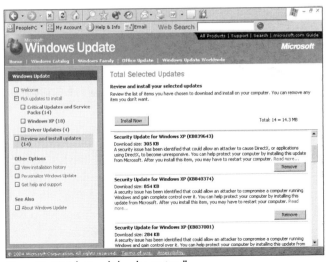

Figure 11-12: Selecting which updates to install

Set File Attributes

1. Locate the file that you want to modify by using Windows Explorer. (Choose Start⇨All Programs⇨ Accessories⇨Windows Explorer.)

2. Right-click the file and choose Properties.

3. In the resulting *Filename* Properties dialog box, shown in Figure 11-13, click the General tab.

4. Select the Read-Only or Hidden check boxes.

5. Click OK to accept the new settings.

 If you want to see the files that you've marked as hidden, go to the file or folder location (for example, in the My Documents folder or by using Windows Explorer) and choose Tools⇨Folder Options. Click the View tab to display it. In the Advanced Settings area, select the Show Hidden Files and Folders option and click OK.

Figure 11-13: The *Filename* Properties dialog box

Extending Windows XP Functionality with Service Pack 2

*1*n the world of computers, new security threats appear all the time, and improvements to operating systems occur to brainy people ensconced in software company offices. As a result, sometime in the second half of 2004 Microsoft issued Service Pack 2. SP2 (as it's affectionately known) is installed as an interim update to Windows XP; that means it's not really a new version of the operating system, but it does add features and functionality, mainly in the area of computer security.

A word of advice: SP2 can take a while to download from Microsoft's Web site (like a few hours), so you might want to order it on CD. When you run the install program, it's pretty seamless — after it starts loading files, all you have to do is go away for a few hours. When you come back and reboot your computer, the SP2 features are in place.

When you boot up, you see a message about turning on Automatic Updates, which is a good thing to do to update security features from Microsoft going forward. Then occasionally new windows appear. For example, Security Center appears asking you to review some new security settings, or the Information Bar in Internet Explorer keeps you informed about Internet events (such as attempted downloads) that could pose security threats. But rest assured that, for the most part, functionality of Windows XP is just as I've stated it in the rest of this book.

Here, then, are the key features of SP2.

Chapter 12

Get ready to . . .

Set Up Pop-Up Blocker

1. With Internet Explorer open, choose Tools➪Pop-Up Blocker➪Pop-Up Blocker Settings.

2. In the Pop-Up Blocker Settings dialog box, shown in Figure 12-1, enter a URL in the Address of Web Site to Allow text box.

3. Click Add. You can also do the following:

   • Deselect the Play a Sound When a Pop-Up Is Blocked check box, so that the sound doesn't play every time a pop-up is blocked.

   • Deselect the Show Information Bar When a Pop-up is Blocked check box, so the Information Bar doesn't appear when a pop-up is blocked.

   • Select another level from the Filter Level drop-down list. You can block all pop-ups.

4. Click the Close button to close the dialog box.

Warning: Blocking all pop-up windows might not be your best choice. Why? Although pop-up windows are often used for advertising products that you don't want or even find embarrassing, some pop-ups are good. For example, if you click a link that opens a photograph in a larger version, it could be set up to use a pop-up window. Or, if you click to see a price list, it might also be meant to appear in a pop-up. My advice is to stick to the medium pop-up-filter level of blocking.

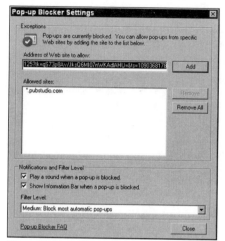

Figure 12-1: The Pop-Up Blocker Settings dialog box

If you got a notification through the Information Bar that a pop-up has been blocked, you can choose to see what you're missing. Click the Information Bar when it appears, and choose Show Blocked Pop-Up from the shortcut menu. From the information that's displayed, you can then decide if you want to block that content or not.

If you've made settings to block all pop-ups and still see one now and then, check in the IE Internet Options dialog box (choose Tools➪Internet Options) on the Privacy tab. Any sites that you've specified in the Trusted Sites category here are allowed to display pop-ups.

Stop the Information Bar from Blocking File and Software Downloads

1. With Internet Explorer open, choose Tools⇨Internet Options, and click the Security tab.

2. On the Security Tab shown in Figure 12-2, click the Custom Level button.

3. In the Security Settings dialog box, shown in Figure 12-3, you can change one of two options:

   • In the Downloads section, select the Enable radio button for Automatic Prompting for File Downloads.

   • In the Active X Controls and Plug-Ins section, shown in Figure 12-3, select the Enable radio button for the Automatic Prompting for Active X Controls.

4. Click OK in the Security Settings dialog box, and then click OK in the Internet Options dialog box to close both dialog boxes and save the new settings.

 What might the Information Bar do when it's enabled? It might stop a site from installing an ActiveX control on your computer, or block downloading of files to your computer (without your permission) that might be used to track your online activities. By blocking ActiveX controls, some Web pages might not display properly. The Information Bar settings might also stop you from viewing content because the site's content and its security information don't match. This is all meant to protect you, but in practice, you might find some of this blocking interfering with you doing what you need to online. Microsoft urges you to leave all settings in place, but you might have to play around with them to get things right for the way you work on the Web.

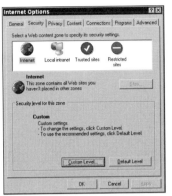

Figure 12-2: The Internet Options dialog box, Security tab

 You might search high and low for the Information Bar, but you can't display it. It turns on only when a Web site that you visit tries to install an ActiveX control on your computer, open a pop-up window, download a file (one you haven't asked to have downloaded), or run ActiveX controls or content on your computer.

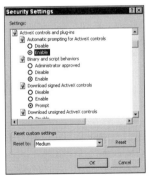

Figure 12-3: The Security Settings dialog box

Disable or Update Add-Ons

1. Choose Tools⇨Manage Add-Ons.

2. In the Manage Add-Ons dialog box, shown in Figure 12-4, click an add-on listed there.

3. To disable the add-on, click the Disable radio button in the Settings area.

4. If the add-on isn't the most current version, the Update button in the Update section is available. Click it and you might see a few different things, including:

   • A dialog box asking whether you trust the security on the site that IE has to visit to update the add-on. (Click Yes or No.)

   • A message indicating the add-on is updating (see Figure 12-5).

   • A message indicating that no update to the add-on is available.

5. Click OK to close the dialog box.

 Add-ons add some function to your Web browser; for example, a search engine toolbar or stock ticker. You might be happy to have some add-ons, but not all. Or you might want to periodically update an add-on.

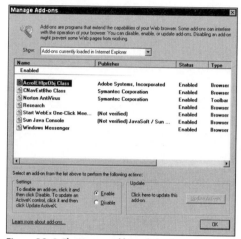

Figure 12-4: The Manage Add-Ons dialog box

 Where did all these add-ons come from, you ask? In some cases, you have specifically given permission to a Web site to install an add-on. Other add-ons appear because you gave permission for a site to download any add-ons it likes to your computer. (I know, you figure you'd have to be crazy to do that, but it was probably 3 a.m. and you were zonked out on one too many Minesweeper games.) Sometimes add-ons are included with other programs you download, all unbeknownst to you. And finally, Windows XP itself installs some add-ons on your computer when you update Windows or browse the Web.

Figure 12-5: Updating in progress

View Your Security Settings in Windows Security Center

1. Choose Start⇨Control Panel and click the Security Center link.

2. In the Windows Security Center shown in Figure 12-6, click the double-arrow buttons next to each item to review the current settings, including:

    - **Firewall:** Tells you whether the Windows Firewall feature is enabled (On) or disabled (Off).

    - **Automatic Updates:** Shows whether the Windows Automatic Updates feature is set to be on or off at the recommended setting.

    - **Virus Protection:** Shows what virus protection software is currently active on your computer (if any).

3. To change a setting, click the Change the Way Security Center Alerts Me link in the Resources area on the left side of the Security Center.

4. In the Alert Settings dialog box (see Figure 12-7), select any check box to enable or disable one of the three settings that I describe in Step 2.

5. Click OK to save the settings, and then click the Close button in the Windows Security Center to close it.

 To manage more detail for each of the three settings in the Windows Security Center, click a link in the Manage Security Settings For area at the bottom of the Security Center window. The dialog boxes that you access from these links typically let you make choices somewhere between enabled and disabled; for example, you might set up Automatic Update to allow downloads but let you choose when they're installed.

Figure 12-6: The Windows Security Center

 How, exactly, does a firewall work? A firewall stops unauthorized users from accessing your system. Windows Firewall in SP2 is turned on by default. When an antivirus program spots virus programs that have gotten onto your computer, a firewall keeps people from coming in your back door who have no business being there, and who, if they gained access, might leave a virus or snoop around.

Figure 12-7: The Alert Settings dialog box

Set Up Windows Firewall Exceptions

1. Choose Start⇨My Network Places, and click the View Network Connections link.

2. In the Network Connections window, click the Change Windows Firewall Settings link.

3. In the Windows Firewall dialog box, click the Exceptions tab, shown in Figure 12-8.

4. Click the Add Program button.

5. In the Add a Program dialog box (see Figure 12-9), select a program that you want to allow communications with, and then click OK.

6. Now you are returned to the Exceptions tab of the Windows Firewall dialog box, where, if you don't want to be notified when Windows Firewall blocks access to a program, you should deselect the Display a Notification When Windows Firewall Blocks a Program check box.

7. Click the OK button to save the new settings.

 Why would you want to allow a program to communicate with your computer? Well, imagine that you play games over the Internet all the time. You might decide to accept the risk of allowing communication through the Zone.com online gaming service, for example. Through trial and sometimes disastrous error, you might have to figure out how to keep a balance between staying secure and taking advantage of all the benefits that the Internet has to offer.

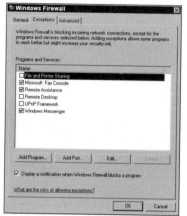

Figure 12-8: Windows Firewall dialog box, Exceptions tab

 If you've played around with the firewall settings and decided you'd rather trust Microsoft's defaults, you can return Windows Firewall to its default settings. To do so, in the Windows Firewall Settings dialog box shown in Figure 12-8, click the Advanced tab, and click the Restore Defaults button.

Figure 12-9: The Add a Program dialog box

Block External Content in HTML Messages in Outlook Express

1. Choose Start⇨Outlook Express.

2. Choose Tools⇨Options.

3. In the Options dialog box, click the Security tab to display it (see Figure 12-10).

4. Select the Block Images and Other External Content in HTML E-Mail check box.

5. Click OK to save the setting.

 You might wonder what that red X in your e-mail is. If you have blocked images and other types of content from being displayed in HTML e-mail messages, such items are replaced by the red X.

 If you forward or reply to a message that includes blocked content, Windows downloads the content and includes it in the forwarded message.

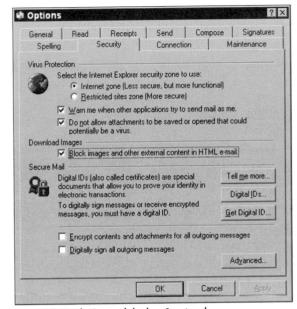

Figure 12-10: The Options dialog box, Security tab

 To download blocked content that you want to get (for example, if you signed up for how-to tips from a software provider), you can click the Information Bar, which appears under the Address Bar to alert you that content has been blocked.

Manage Automatic Updates

1. Choose Start➪Control Panel, click the Performance and Maintenance link, and then click the System link.

2. In the System Properties dialog box, click the Automatic Updates tab to display it (see Figure 12-11).

3. Select one of the four radio buttons to specify how you want to manage updates:

   • **The Automatic option** downloads and installs updates at the specified frequency and time of day you select from the two drop down boxes here.

   • **The Download Updates For Me option** lets updates be downloaded but not installed until you choose to do so.

   • **The Notify Me option** causes Windows to send you a message that there are downloads, but they are not downloaded nor installed.

   • **The Turn Off Automatic Updates option** turns this feature off entirely. To get updates you would then have to go to the Windows Update Web site, which you can do by clicking the link here.

4. Click OK.

 When Windows is downloading updates to your computer, it doesn't interrupt your work. The download happens in the background of other work you're doing, and you can even download other files at the same time.

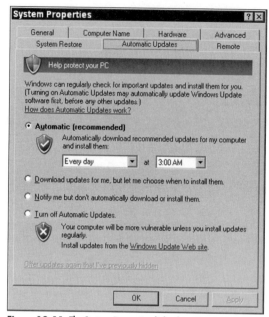

Figure 12-11: The System Properties dialog box, Automatic Updates tab

 You can also go to the Windows Update Web site by opening the Help & Support Center (choose Start➪Help and Support) and clicking the Windows Update link in the Resources area on the left. Windows Update is also listed when you choose Start➪All Programs.

 If you happen to disconnect or lose your connection to the Internet before an update finishes downloading, don't panic. Next time you go online, Windows Update completes the download right from where you left off.

Part V
Fixing Common Problems

Troubleshooting Hardware Problems

Computer hardware, like your CPU and printer, is cool. Hardware is gad-getry that hums and beeps and looks neat on your desktop. But when hardware goes wrong, you might be tempted to throw it out the window. Don't do that — think of all the money you spent on it. Instead, use Windows to isolate and troubleshoot the problem.

Windows has several features that help you diagnose and treat the sickest hardware, including:

➡ A Printing Troubleshooter that walks you through a wizard-like inter-face to figure out what the printer problem is and fix it.

➡ A Disk Cleanup feature that checks your hard drive for problems that could be causing poor performance, such as bad sectors on the drive or bits of stray data that could simply be thrown away, freeing up space and helping your system to perform better.

➡ Modem diagnostics that query your modem to be sure that it's con-nected, configured, and performing properly.

➡ A Hardware Troubleshooter feature in the Windows Help and Support Center that walks you through choices to isolate and fix a variety of hardware problems.

➡ The ability to quickly and easily update hardware drivers that might help your hardware perform optimally.

Troubleshoot a Printer Problem

1. Choose Start➪Control Panel➪Printers and Other Hardware➪Printers and Faxes. In the window that appears, click the Printing link in the Troubleshooter area.

2. In the window that appears (see Figure 13-1), select the problem that's closest to what you're experiencing (for example, you're having trouble installing a printer). Click Next.

3. What appears at this point differs depending on the printing problem that you're experiencing, but typically the Printing Troubleshooter gives you some instructions for procedures to try, such as printing a test page and then selecting among items based on your results (see Figure 13-2 for an example). So, for example, you might be told to:

    -   Try to print a test page and then select the option that says that you can print from WordPad or NotePad, but not from the original application, and click Next.

    -   Reinstall your printer driver.

    -   Use TrueType fonts to format your document, which could cause your text to print correctly.

4. In the resulting windows, continue to try procedures and indicate the results, clicking Next to display the troubleshooter's next suggestions, until you isolate and solve the problem.

5. Click the Close button in the upper-right corner to close the Troubleshooter.

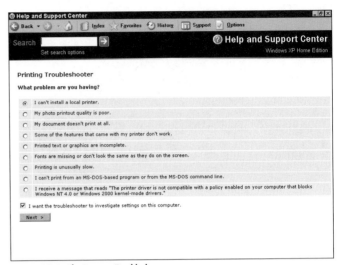

Figure 13-1: The Printing Troubleshooter

Figure 13-2: The Printing Troubleshooter in action

Use Disk Defragmenter to Check a Hard Drive for Errors

1. Choose Start➪All Programs➪Accessories➪System Tools➪Disk Defragmenter.

2. In the Disk Defragmenter window (see Figure 13-3), click your hard drive (usually drive C:) and then click the Analyze button. Disk Defragmenter analyzes the drive.

3. To view the resulting report (see Figure 13-4), click the View Report button in the dialog box that appears. Click the Close button to close the report. If the analysis recommends that you proceed, click the Defragment button. The procedure runs and cleans up your hard drive, consolidating fragmented files to improve performance.

 Another tool that you can use to check your hard drive for potentially troublesome problems is Disk Cleanup. (Choose Start➪All Programs➪Accessories➪System Tools➪Disk Cleanup.) Disk Cleanup analyzes how much space you might save by getting rid of unused files, and then offers you the option of getting rid of selected items. Clearing out unused files frees up hard drive space, which could allow your system to operate faster.

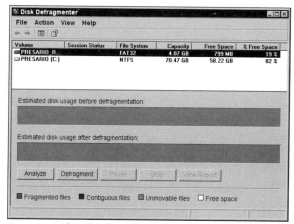

Figure 13-3: The Disk Defragmenter window

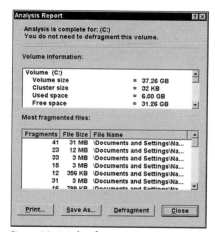

Figure 13-4: Disk Defragmenter's analysis of my hard drive

Run Error Checking to Detect Bad Sectors on a Hard Drive

1. Choose Start➪My Computer.

2. Right-click the disk you want to repair and choose Properties.

3. In the resulting Properties dialog box, click the Tools tab to display it (see Figure 13-5). Click the Check Now button.

4. In the resulting Check Disk dialog box (see Figure 13-6), choose the option you want to use:

   - **Automatically Fix File System Errors:** Note you have to have closed all files in order to run this option.

   - **Scan for and Attempt Recovery of Bad Sectors:** If you choose this, it also automatically fixes any errors found, so you don't need to select the first option as well.

5. Click Start.

 What exactly is a file system error? The file system is the basic structure of an operating system that deals with how system files are named, stored, and organized. If there's an error, Windows might have trouble locating a file, which can cause you a variety of functional problems.

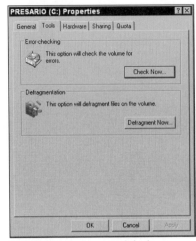

Figure 13-5: The Properties dialog box, Tools tab

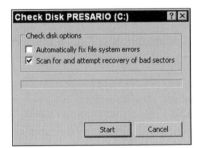

Figure 13-6: The Check Disk dialog box

Perform Modem Diagnostics

1. Choose Start⇨Control Panel⇨Phone and Modem Options.

2. In the resulting dialog box (see Figure 13-7), click the Modems tab and then the Properties button. Click the Troubleshoot button on the General tab of the Properties dialog box that appears.

3. In the resulting Modem Troubleshooter window, select the description that best matches the problems that you're experiencing, and then click Next.

4. The information that appears differs depending on the modem problem you're experiencing, but typically the Modem Troubleshooter gives you some instructions and choices for procedures to try (see Figure 13-8 for an example).

5. Click Next to proceed through these screens until you've isolated the problem.

6. Find the problem and click the Close button in the upper-right corner of the Troubleshooter to close it.

 When using any Windows troubleshooter, I recommend leaving the I Want the Troubleshooter to Investigate Settings on this Computer check box in the initial window selected. This doesn't open you up to any online Tom, Dick, or Mary coming in and looking over your system; it simply allows the troubleshooter to check certain settings within your system. This is faster than having to check them yourself, so it's a good thing to do.

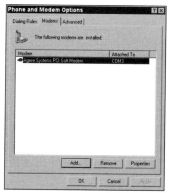

Figure 13-7: The Phone and Modem Options dialog box, Modem tab

Figure 13-8: The Modem Troubleshooter

Use the Hardware Troubleshooter

1. Choose Start⇨Help and Support⇨Hardware⇨Fixing a Hardware Problem⇨Hardware Troubleshooter.

2. In the resulting Hardware Troubleshooter window shown in Figure 13-9, select the item that most closely matches the problem that you're having, and click Next.

3. In the resulting window, follow the instructions that relate to your problem. (Figure 13-10 shows instructions for a display adapter problem as an example.)

4. If the resulting information solves the problem, select Yes, This Solves the Problem. Select No, I Still Have a Problem if the information doesn't help. Click Next.

5. When you've solved the problem, click the Close button to close the Hardware Troubleshooter.

 If when you're following the Hardware Troubleshooter you decide that you've taken the wrong path somewhere or should have tried an alternate suggested procedure, quickly go back and start again by clicking the Start Over button on any Troubleshooter screen. You can also go back screen by screen by clicking the Back button.

 Occasionally you'll see a link in a troubleshooter sequence that will take you to a different troubleshooter. For example, if you started troubleshooting a CD drive and indicated you could use data files but not play audio files from the drive, a Sound Troubleshooter link might be offered. Just be aware that if you click this link, you'll leave the troubleshooter you're in and have to start it all over again if the new link doesn't solve your problem.

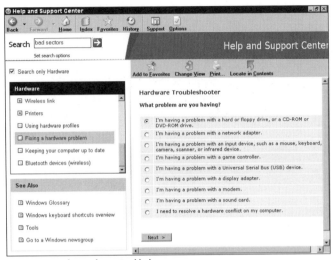

Figure 13-9: The Hardware Troubleshooter

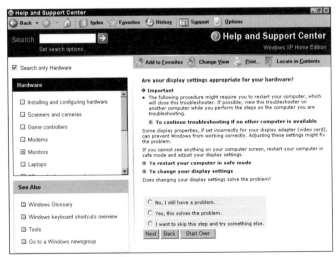

Figure 13-10: The Help and Support Center

Update a Driver

1. Put the CD or floppy disk with the updated driver on it in the appropriate drive of your computer or download a driver onto your hard drive from the Internet.

2. Choose Start⇨Control Panel⇨System.

3. In the resulting System Properties dialog box, click the Hardware tab to display it and then click the Device Manager button (see Figure 13-11).

4. In the resulting window, click the plus sign next to any hardware item to display the installed hardware, and then click a hardware item and choose Action⇨Update Driver from the menu bar.

5. In the Hardware Update Wizard window (see Figure 13-12), you can choose to

   • Install the driver automatically (which sends Windows scurrying around your hard drive to locate it).

   • Install it from a specific source, such as a CD-ROM. The next window that appears provides ways to search removable media such as a floppy disk or CD, or to specify a location on your computer.

6. Follow the rest of the steps indicated by the wizard based on your choices to update your driver. When the wizard is done, click Finish.

 In some cases, you have to reboot your computer to give Windows a chance to load the new driver. Choose Start⇨Turn Off Computer. In the resulting Turn Off Computer dialog box, click the Restart button to reboot your system. The driver should now, by the magic of Windows' Plug-and-Play feature that automatically detects new hardware, be working.

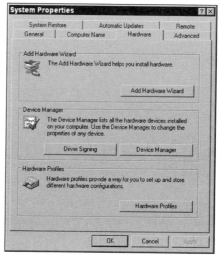

Figure 13-11: The System Properties dialog box

Figure 13-12: The Hardware Update Wizard

Reinstall a Corrupted Driver

1. Locate the device associated with the corrupted driver and disconnect it from your computer.

2. Turn off the device.

3. Choose Start⇨Control Panel⇨System.

4. In the System Properties dialog box, click the Hardware tab to display it (see Figure 13-13) and then click the Device Manager button.

5. In the resulting window (see Figure 13-14), choose the category relating to your device. Right-click the specific device, and then choose Uninstall from the pop-up menu.

6. When the uninstall procedure is complete, restart your computer, reconnect the device and turn it on. At this point you can do a couple of things to reinstall the driver:

   • Insert a disc containing the driver and run the installation from that disc. This process usually involves double-clicking on a setup.exe file from Windows Explorer.

   • Allow the Plug-and-Play feature of Windows to automatically detect and install the driver for you.

 If Plug-and-Play doesn't install the driver automatically and you don't have it on a disc, you can use the Add Hardware Wizard to install it. Choose Start⇨Control Panel⇨Add Hardware to call up the Add Hardware Wizard.

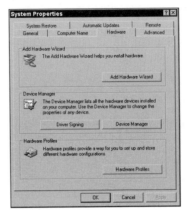

Figure 13-13: The System Properties dialog box, Hardware tab

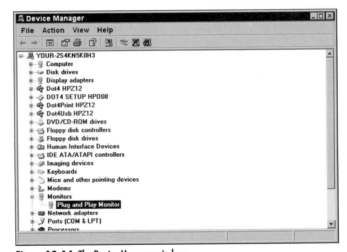

Figure 13-14: The Device Manager window

Troubleshooting Software Problems

A ll the wonderful hardware that you've spent your hard-earned money on doesn't mean a thing if the software driving it goes flooey. If any programs cause your system to *crash* (meaning it freezes up so there's less action on your screen than on a loser's prom night), you can try a variety of tasks to fix it. In this chapter, you find out how to recover when the following problems occur:

→ When a program crashes, you can simply shut that program down by using the Windows Task Manager. This utility keeps track of all the programs and processes that are running on your computer.

→ If you've got problems and Windows isn't responding, sometimes it helps to restart in Safe Mode, which requires only basic files and drivers. Restarting in Safe Mode often allows you to troubleshoot what's going on, and you can restart Windows in its regular mode after the problem is solved.

→ Use the System Restore feature to first create a *system restore point* (a point in time when your settings and programs all seem to be humming along just fine) and then restore Windows to that point when trouble hits.

→ If all else fails, you might have to reformat an entire drive. This wipes all information from the drive, and if it's the hard drive that you reformat, you have to start again by reloading the operating system and all your software.

→ Sometimes you just have to run older programs on Windows XP, but to avoid compatibility issues that could crash your system, try running Program Compatibility Wizard to test your program first.

Get ready to . . .

Shut Down a Non-Responsive Application

1. Press Ctrl+Alt+Del.

2. In the Windows Task Manager dialog box (see Figure 14-1), select the application that you were in when your system stopped responding.

3. Click the End Task button.

4. In the resulting dialog box (see Figure 14-2), the Windows Task Manager tells you that the application isn't responding and asks whether you want to shut it down now. Click the End Now button.

 If pressing Ctrl+Alt+Del doesn't bring up the Task Manager, you're in bigger trouble than you thought. Press Ctrl+Alt+Del once again, and Windows reboots. Sometimes this solves the problem, and you can get right back to work. Note that some applications use an Auto Save feature that keeps an interim version of the document that you were working in and you might be able to save some of your work by opening that last-saved version. Other programs don't have such a safety net, and you simply lose whatever changes you made to your document since the last time you last saved it. The moral? Save, and save often.

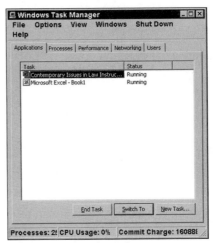

Figure 14-1: The Windows Task Manager

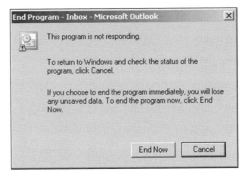

Figure 14-2: A non-responsive program message

Start Windows in Safe Mode

1. Choose Start⇨Turn Off Computer. In the Turn off Computer dialog box (see Figure 14-3), click the Restart button to reboot your system.

2. When the computer starts to reboot (the screen goes black), begin pressing F8.

3. In the resulting plain vanilla text-based screen, press the up or down arrow key to select the Safe Mode option from the list and press Enter.

4. On the resulting screen, use the up and down arrow keys to select the Windows XP operating system, or type the number of that choice, and press Enter.

5. In the resulting dialog box, which explains what Safe Mode is and the option of running System Restore, click Yes to open Windows XP Safe Mode, as shown if Figure 14 4.

6. Use the tools in the Control Panel and the Help and Support system to figure out your problem, make changes, and then restart. When you restart again (repeat Step 1), you start in the standard Windows XP mode.

 When you reboot and press F8 as in Step 2, you're in the old text-based world that users of the DOS operating system remember. It's scary out there — your mouse doesn't work a lick and no fun sounds or cool graphics exist to sooth you. In fact, DOS is the reason the whole For Dummies series started, because *everybody* felt like a dummy using it, me included. Just use your arrow keys to get around, and press Enter to make selections. You're back in Windows-land soon. . . .

Figure 14-3: The Turn Off Computer dialog box

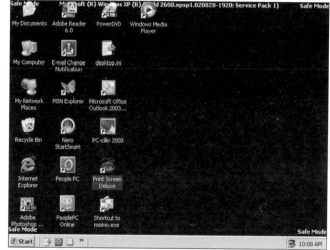

Figure 14-4: Windows XP running in Safe Mode

Create a System Restore Point

1. Choose Start⇨All Programs⇨Accessories⇨System Tools⇨ System Restore.

2. Select the Create a Restore Point radio button and then click Next.

3. In the resulting dialog box (see Figure 14-5), fill in the Restore Point Description text box; this description is helpful if you create multiple restore points and want to identify the correct one. The current date is usually your best bet.

4. Click the Create button, and the system restore point is created and is available to you when you run a System Restore (see Figure 14-6).

 Every once in a while, when you install some software and make some new settings in Windows and things seem to be running just fine, create a system restore point. It's good computer practice, just like backing up your files, only you're backing up your settings. Once a month or once every couple months works for most people, but if you frequently make changes, create a system restore point more often.

 A more drastic option to System Restore is to run the system recovery disc that probably came with your computer. However, system recovery essentially puts your computer right back to the configuration it had when it was carried out of the factory. That means you lose any software you've installed and documents you've created since you began to use it. A good argument for creating system restore points on a regular basis, don't you think?

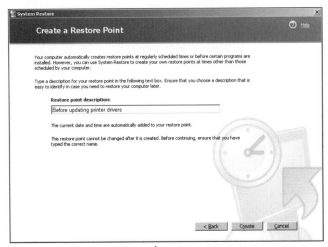

Figure 14-5: A system restore point description

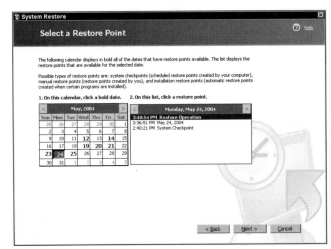

Figure 14-6: A list of possible system restore points

Restore the Windows System

1. Choose Start➪All Programs➪Accessories➪System Tools➪ System Restore.

2. In the System Restore dialog box (see Figure 14-7), accept the default option of Restore My Computer to an Earlier Time by clicking Next.

3. In the resulting dialog box, click the arrow keys on the right or left of the calendar to search the months and locate the system restore point that you want to use. (Refer to Figure 14-6.)

4. Select the system restore point that you want to use, and then click Next.

5. As prompted by the Confirm Restore Point Selection dialog box, shown in Figure 14-8, shut down any running programs. When you're ready, click Next.

6. The system goes through a shutdown and restart sequence, and then displays a dialog box that informs you that the System Restore has occurred.

7. Click OK to close it.

 System Restore doesn't get rid of files that you've saved, so you don't lose your Ph.D. dissertation. System Restore simply reverts to Windows settings as of the Restore Point. This can help if you or some piece of installed software made a setting that is causing some conflict in your system that makes your computer sluggish or prone to crashes.

 If you restore to a time before you installed Service Pack 2, you might have to reinstall the whole thing to keep the benefits it offers. See Chapter 12 for more about SP2.

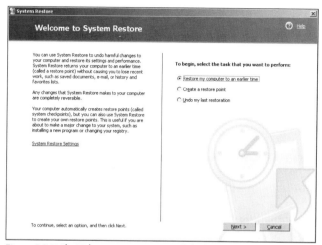

Figure 14-7: The Welcome to System Restore dialog box

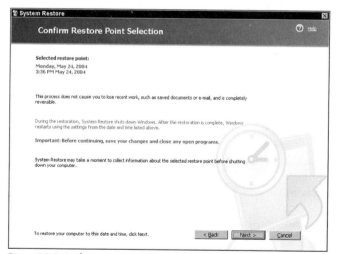

Figure 14-8: Ready to run a System Restore

Reformat a Drive

1. Assuming your system is still functional enough to let you do so, backup everything you can find (documents, photos, graphics, saved e-mails, updates, drivers, and so on; don't worry about software programs because you'll have to reinstall those, anyway) and close all applications.

2. Choose Start⇨Control Panel⇨Administrative Tools.

3. In the Administrative Tools window (see Figure 14-9), double-click Computer Management.

4. In the resulting Computer Management window (see Figure 14-10), click Disk Management (in the left pane). Right-click the drive or partition that you want to reformat (in the right pane), and then choose Format from the shortcut menu that appears.

5. In the resulting dialog box, select the options you want, and then click OK.

 Backing up files before running any system maintenance procedure is a good idea. Better safe than sorry. For more about how to back up files, see Chapter 8.

 I can't stress strongly enough: Before you reformat a drive you should backup everything you can, including drivers or updates to software that you've sat through tedious minutes (or hours) to download from the Web. You don't want to have to spend all that download time all over again to get yourself up to speed. This goes double if you installed Windows Service Pack 2: If you've gone through the few hours it takes to download and install, you don't want to have to revisit that experience, right?

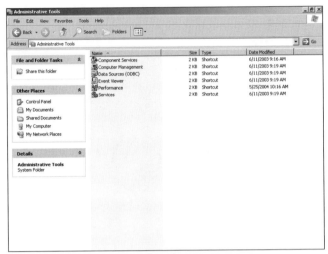

Figure 14-9: The Administrative Tools window

 Note that you have to be logged on as the head honcho, the system administrator, to perform these steps. And it's worth repeating: Reformatting a drive wipes *everything* off of it, so be sure that's what you want to do before you do it.

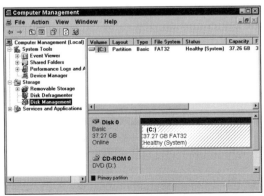

Figure 14-10: The Computer Management window

Getting Help

*W*ith so many Windows features, you're bound to run into something that doesn't work right or isn't easy to figure out (and that this book doesn't cover) at some point. That's when you need to call on the resources that Microsoft provides to help you out.

Through the Help and Support Center, you can get help in various ways, including the following:

➥ **Access information that's stored in the Help system database:** Drill down from one topic to another or use a powerful search mechanism.

➥ **Use preset help tasks and tutorials:** Get right where you need to go to watch a demonstration or follow a wizard to solve your problem step by step.

➥ **Get help from your fellow Windows users:** Tap into information exchanged by users in newsgroup discussions or by using a little feature called Remote Assistance, which allows you to let another user take over your computer from a distance (via the Internet) and figure out your problem for you.

➥ **Bite the bullet and pay for it:** Microsoft offers some help for free (for example, help for installing software that you paid good money for), but some help comes for a price. When you can't find help anywhere else, you might want to consider forking over a few hard-earned bucks for this option.

Chapter
15

Get ready to . . .

Explore Help Topics

1. Choose Start⇨Help and Support to open the Support Center, as shown in Figure 15-1. *Note:* If your copy of Windows came built into your computer, some computer manufacturers, such as Hewlett-Packard, customize this center to add information that's specific to your computer system.

2. Click a Help Topic link in the Pick a Help Topic column to display the next level of options. Along the left side of the following screen, you see major topics listed, some of them with a plus sign to the left.

3. Click any of the plus signs to expand the topic and see a list of subtopics. Eventually you get down to the deepest level of detailed subtopics, as shown in Figure 15-2.

4. Click a topic in the Pick a Task list on the right to display the topic. When you get to this level, you might find additional links to display information about various aspects of this topic, links within the help text that you can click to get background information or definitions of terms, and a Related Topics area where you click links to take you to other information related to this topic.

5. When you finish reading about the topic(s) that you need help with, click the Close button to close the Help and Support Center window.

 At the topic level, a See Also list box is available on the left that provides links to often useful resources. For example, from any list of topics you can access a glossary of computer terms that might help you understand what's being explained by the Help and Support Center, or you can click a link to go to a related newsgroup, or get a list of Windows keystroke shortcuts.

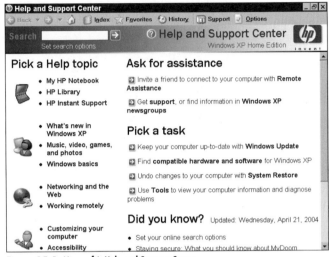

Figure 15-1: Microsoft's Help and Support Center

Figure 15-2: Detailed level help topics

Search for Help

1. Open the Help and Support Center.

2. Enter a search term in the Search box and click the Start Searching button. Search results, such as those shown in Figure 15-3, appear.

3. Explore the results by clicking various links in the Search Results area on the left. These links offer a few different types of results:

   - The Suggested Topics list offers relevent help topics, articles, and tutorials related to your search.

   - The Full-Text Search Matches area lists links to more help topics.

   - The Microsoft Knowledge Base list offers related technical articles from Microsoft.

4. Click any item to display it. If you have no luck, enter a different search term in the Search text box and start again.

5. To change how Search operates, click the Set search options link under the Search text box. You can change the following settings:

   - Change the number of results returned in the Return Up To text box at the top. (The default is 15 as shown in Figure 15-4.)

   - Select the Turn on Search Highlight check box to turn this feature on and off.

   - Select a check box to select or deselect one of the three search results options.

6. In the Search For drop-down list, choose how the search should be performed; for example, based on all words in the search phrase, based on any of the words, or only by the exact phrase you've entered.

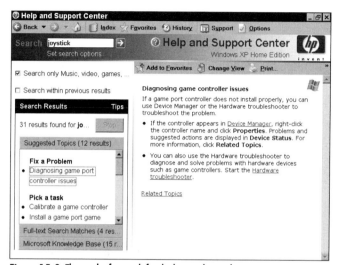

Figure 15-3: The result of a search for the keyword joystick

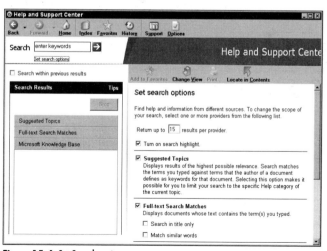

Figure 15-4: Set Search options

Run a Tutorial

1. Open the Help and Support Center. You can locate tutorials here in a couple ways:

   - Enter the word *tutorial* in the Search text box and click the arrow button. Links to the first 15 tutorials appear. (Fifteen is the default number of search results.) Click a link to run a tutorial.

   - When you run a search, the Suggested Topics section of the results typically divides into two sections: Pick a Task; and Overviews, Articles and Tutorials. Any item in the second area that begins with the word *Practice* is a tutorial.

2. Click a tutorial link to run it. It runs, opening a window that plays images along with an audio narration and a toolbar. Do one of the following:

   - When you're instructed to by the narration, perform an action, such as clicking a link in the tutorial window.

   - Use the tutorial toolbar, shown in Figure 15-5, to navigate through the tutorial. For example, use the Previous Topic, Jump Back, Jump Ahead, or Next Topic buttons to move through the tutorial content, and use the Pause and Stop buttons to take a break from the tutorial or stop it from running.

   - Use the tutorial toolbar to get more help with the More Information, Glossary, Tip, and Help buttons.

   - Close a tutorial by clicking the Close button in the tutorial window.

Figure 15-5: A Windows tutorial

 Tutorials are played by using the Macromedia Flash Player. To modify the way the player works, when a tutorial first begins, right click the tutorial screen and choose Settings. These settings control privacy, microphone recording volume, camera settings, and how much storage space is used on your hard drive to play the tutorials. To adjust playback volume, click the volume control on the Windows taskbar and move the sliders up and down to make the sound louder or softer.

Find Information in Newsgroups

1. Open the Help and Support Center and then click a topic to display it.

2. In the See Also section of the results, click the Go to a Windows Newsgroup link. *Note:* You might need to be connected to the Internet before this feature works, or Windows might connect you automatically. A listing of newsgroups appears, as shown in Figure 15-6.

3. Click a link for a newsgroup that seems to match your interest or problem. Click the Web-Based Reader link to see a browser-type interface; click the Newsreader link to display the discussion topics in Outlook Express. A list of discussions appears.

4. Click a topic to display a list of all postings under it. Click a posting to display it in the lower pane, as shown in Figure 15-7. Perform any of the following actions to participate in the newsgroup:

    *   **Post a new message:** Click the New button, and enter your Display Name, Subject, and Message in their respective text boxes, and then click Send.

    *   **Reply to a message in a discussion:** From the list of postings and replies, click the Reply button, fill in the Display Name, Subject, and Message text boxes and then click Send.

 You can also use the Search feature to search for key words or phrases in discussions. Enter a word or phrase in the Search text box, select a discussion to search in the In drop-down list, and then click Go. Relevant messages are displayed; click one to read it.

Figure 15-6: A list of Windows XP newsgroups

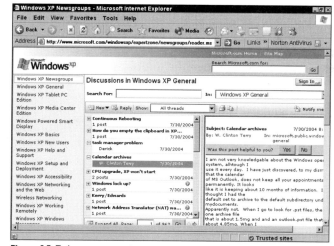

Figure 15-7: A newsgroup posting

Connect to Remote Assistance

1. Open the Help and Support Center. Click the Remote Assistance link in the Ask for Assistance area of the Help and Support Center.

2. On the Remote Assistance page, shown in Figure 15-8, click the Invite someone to help you link. On the page that appears (see Figure 15-9), you can notify somebody that you want them to help you.

3. You can use Windows Messenger or e-mail to invite somebody to help you. For these steps, fill in an e-mail address and click the Invite This Person button.

4. On the E-Mail an Invitation page, enter your name in the From text box and type a message in the Message text box. Then click Continue.

5. On the resulting page, set a time limit on the invitation and require that the recipient use a password to access your computer remotely (a wise security measure). Use the drop-down lists in the Set the Invitation to Expire area to set the timeframe for the invitation to last.

     Setting a time limit to not more than a few hours is a good idea. After all, you don't want somebody trying to log on to your computer unexpectedly two weeks from now when you've already solved the problem some other way.

6. If you want to require a password, enter it and confirm it.

     Remember, it's up to you to let the recipient know the password — it isn't included in your e-mail. If you don't want to use a password, be sure to deselect the check box for this option before continuing.

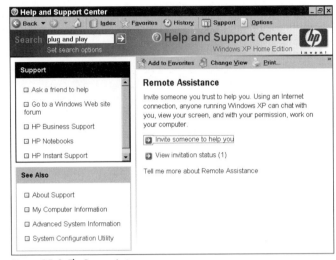

Figure 15-8: The Remote Assistance page

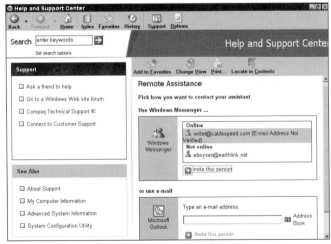

Figure 15-9: Invite help by instant message or e-mail

7. Click the Send Invitation button. The recipient receives an e-mail that includes any message you entered, a standard Remote Assistance message, and a link to further instructions, as shown in Figure 15-10.

8. At this point, the recipient should open the `MsRC Incident` file attached to the e-mail, and if prompted, open it rather than save it. The recipient clicks Yes to accept the invitation and then enters a password, if required.

9. Now, if you're online, you see a message from your remote buddy asking whether you want this person to view your screen and chat, and you can initiate the connection by clicking Yes. You can chat online, and your friend can even take over your mouse and keyboard and work with your computer (with your permission) by using the tools shown in Figure 15-11. For example, you can

- Use the Take Control/Stop Control button to allow the person to take over your system (and stop them when their assistance is no longer needed).

- Enter a message and click Send to communicate.

- Use the Send a File button to share files that might help or be causing problems for you.

10. When you're done with your session, click the Disconnect button, and it is ended.

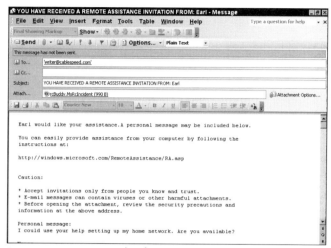

Figure 15-10: An invitation asking for assistance

Figure 15-11: The control screen for a Remote Assistance session

Change Help and Support Center Options

1. Open the Help and Support Center and click the Options button on the toolbar.

2. In the window that appears (see Figure 15-12), click the Change Help and Support Center Options link.

3. When your options appear (see Figure 15-13), play with these settings to do the following:

   • Customize what displays on the Navigation bar (the set of tools across the top of each Help and Support Center screen) by selecting the Show Favorites on Navigation Bar check box or the Show History on Navigation bar check box.

   • Modify the size of text displayed in the Help and Support Center by selecting the Small, Medium, or Large option button.

   • Change the way icons and their text labels are displayed in the Navigation bar by selecting one of the option buttons. Essentially, you can show all labels, show only default labels, or show no labels at all (only the icons themselves).

4. Your new settings take effect immediately; click the Close button or navigate to another area of the Help and Support Center.

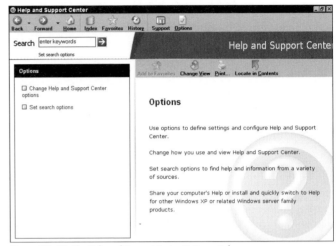

Figure 15-12: The Help and Support Center Options window

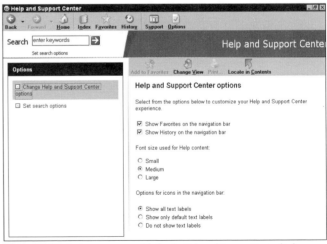

Figure 15-13: Options you can modify for the Help and Support Center display

Get Paid Support from Microsoft

1. Open Internet Explorer and go to `http://support.microsoft.com/default.aspx?scid=fh;en-us;prodoffer33a&sd=GN`, the product support Web page shown in Figure 15-14.

2. Click the Start E-Mail Request button to get support by e-mail. You can get support for up to two problems and any installation problem at no charge by using this method. After that, there is a $35 charge for support.

You can also call support for your two free help sessions or installation help by calling 425-635-3311. You can get paid phone support for $35 by calling 800-936-5700, or advanced support for $245 by calling 800-936-4900. Advanced support is for what Microsoft refers to as *mission critical* issues related to software deployment across an enterprise or larger network issues.

Note: Phone support is available Monday through Friday from 5 a.m. to 9 p.m., and Saturday and Sunday from 6 a.m. to 3 p.m. Even if you're using the free sessions, don't forget that phone charges apply, and unless you live next door to Microsoft, they could add up to a tidy sum for a typical support session. (The last one I had returned a whopping 46-minute phone charge.)

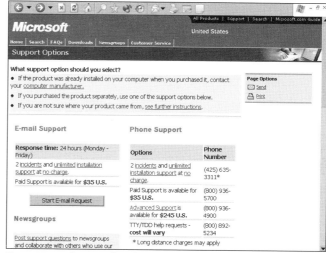

Figure 15-14: The Microsoft Product Support page

If you have installed Service Pack 2, you'll get automatic alerts about potentially damaging conditions or settings that might answer some questions on the fly, and suggest steps to take (like running your antivirus software) to set things right.

Pick a Help Task

1. Open the Help and Support Center window. In the Pick a Task area on the right, click an item. You might see a few different things at this point:

   - Windows might connect you to the Internet, where you can find information on hardware products, on other software products, or on updates for Windows XP (see Figure 15-5).

   - You might be taken to a wizard to help you perform a particular task, such as a System Restore.

2. Follow whatever options Microsoft presents to you for a topic.

 Check out topics provided by Microsoft Product Support Services in the Did You Know? area now and then. They change all the time and might offer up-to-the-minute security alerts or configuration tips.

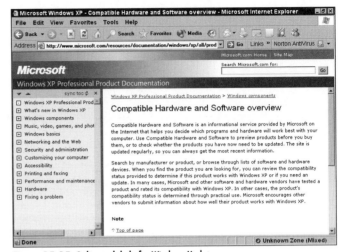

Figure 15-15: Online task help for Windows Updates

Part VI
Fun and Games with Windows

The 5th Wave   By Rich Tennant

MIXING THE FIRST "RUDE AUDIENCE" CD

©RICHTENNANT

"I laid down a general shuffling sound and periodic coughing, some muted talking files, and an awesome ringing cell phone loop."

Playing Games in Windows

All work and no play is just wrong no matter how you look at it. So, Microsoft has built plenty of games into Windows to keep you amused.

Many computer games are essentially virtual versions of games that you already know, such as Solitaire and Checkers. But Windows has added some interesting treats to the mix, like a very graphical Pinball game and computer games like Reversi, which depend to a great extent on on-screen animation.

Altogether, you can access more than a dozen games through Windows, and this chapter gives you a sampling of the best of them. Here's what you can expect:

-   ➡ Traditional card games, such as Solitaire and Spider Solitaire

-   ➡ Games of dexterity, such as Minesweeper, where the goal is to be the fastest, smartest clicker in the West

-   ➡ Internet games that match you up with another player somewhere else on the planet to play a one-on-one game in real time

Play Solitaire

1. Choose Start➪All Programs➪Games➪Solitaire.

2. In the resulting Solitaire window (see Figure 16-1), click a card and drag it to another deck. (You can also move a whole set of cards by clicking and dragging the top card.) You have the following options:

   • If no moves are available, click the stack of cards in the upper-left corner to deal another round of cards.

   • If you move the last card from one of the seven laid-out stacks, leaving only face-down cards, click the face-down cards to flip one up. You can also move a King onto an empty stack.

   • When you reach the end of the stack of cards in the upper-left corner, click them again to redeal the cards that you didn't use the first time.

   • You can play a card in one of two places: either building a stack from King to Ace on the bottom row alternating suits; or starting from Ace in any of the top four slots, placing cards from Ace to King in a single suit.

   • When you complete a set of cards (Ace to King), click and drag it up to one of the four blank deck spots on the top right hand side of the window. If you complete all four sets, you win.

3. To deal a new game, choose Game➪Deal. Unlike life, it's easy to start over with Solitaire!

4. To close Solitaire, click the Close button.

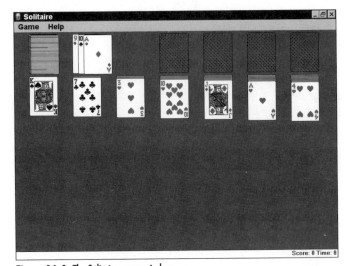

Figure 16-1: The Solitaire game window

 To change settings for the game, choose Game➪Options. The two main settings you'll probably deal with here are Draw (which gives you an option of turning over one or a stack of three cards on each deal) and Scoring (which offers the option of not using scoring at all, or using Standard or Vegas style scoring). Standard scoring starts you off with nothing in the bank and pays you $10 for every card you place. Vegas style is a bit more complex, starting you off with a debit, and crediting you $5 a card in a completed stack, with the object being to come out in the black at the end.

 As with regular old Solitaire, the cards on the seven laid-out stacks have to alternate colors (black and red) and go in descending order from the King down to the Ace.

 Don't like a move you just made? Undo it by choosing Game➪Undo. This works only for the last move, however.

Play FreeCell

1. Choose Start⇨All Programs⇨Games⇨FreeCell.

2. In the resulting FreeCell window, shown in Figure 16-2, choose Game⇨New Game; a new game is dealt and ready to play.

3. Click a card, and then to move it, click a free cell or another card at the bottom of a column. Figure 16-3 shows a game where two free cells are already occupied.

4. To move a stack of cards, click the column of cards, and then click the column to which you want to move it. Note: If you have enough free cells available, the whole stack moves at once (see Figure 16-4).

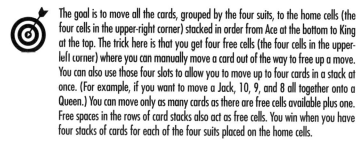

The goal is to move all the cards, grouped by the four suits, to the home cells (the four cells in the upper-right corner) stacked in order from Ace at the bottom to King at the top. The trick here is that you get four free cells (the four cells in the upper-left corner) where you can manually move a card out of the way to free up a move. You can also use those four slots to allow you to move up to four cards in a stack at once. (For example, if you want to move a Jack, 10, 9, and 8 all together onto a Queen.) You can move only as many cards as there are free cells available plus one. Free spaces in the rows of card stacks also act as free cells. You win when you have four stacks of cards for each of the four suits placed on the home cells.

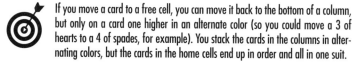

If you move a card to a free cell, you can move it back to the bottom of a column, but only on a card one higher in an alternate color (so you could move a 3 of hearts to a 4 of spades, for example). You stack the cards in the columns in alternating colors, but the cards in the home cells end up in order and all in one suit.

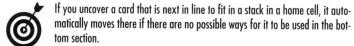

If you uncover a card that is next in line to fit in a stack in a home cell, it automatically moves there if there are no possible ways for it to be used in the bottom section.

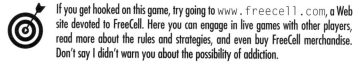

If you get hooked on this game, try going to www.freecell.com, a Web site devoted to FreeCell. Here you can engage in live games with other players, read more about the rules and strategies, and even buy FreeCell merchandise. Don't say I didn't warn you about the possibility of addiction.

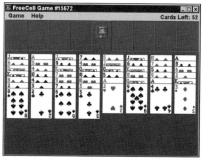

Figure 16-2: A brand new FreeCell game

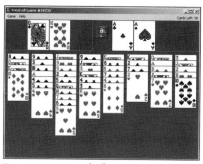

Figure 16-3: Occupied cells

Figure 16-4: A stack ready to be moved

Play Spider Solitaire

1. Choose Start⇨All Programs⇨Games⇨Spider Solitaire.

2. Set the Difficulty level in the dialog box that appears (see Figure 16-5) by selecting one of the following options:

    *   **Easy:** Restricts the game to only one suit.

    *   **Medium:** Limits you to two suits.

    *   **Difficult:** Adds to the game's complexity with all four suits being dealt.

    After you make this choice, click OK.

3. In the resulting set of cards, click a card and drag it to the bottom of another stack or to an empty stack so that you match the same suit in each stack, moving in descending order from King to Ace (see Figure 16-6).

4. Move a card to automatically turn over a new card in the stack.

5. After you complete a set of cards in a suit, those cards are moved off the game area. Remove all the cards in the fewest moves. You can

    *   **Deal a new set of cards:** Choose Deal! or click any of the stacks of cards in the bottom-right corner to deal a new set of cards. (*Note:* You have to have a card on each of the ten stacks before you can deal new ones.)

    *   **Save your game:** Choose Game⇨Save This Game to save your game. To begin a new game, choose Deal! or choose Game⇨Difficulty and select a new difficulty level.

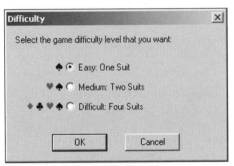

Figure 16-5: Setting the Difficulty level

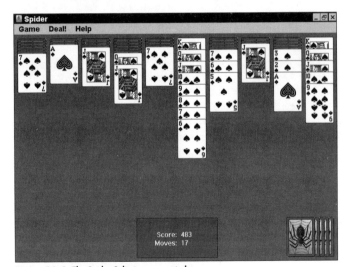

Figure 16-6: The Spider Solitaire game window

- **Change the options:** Choose Game➪Options (see Figure 16-7). These options mainly affect how or whether you save games and open them to continue, and whether the variously annoying or angelic sounds (see Step 4) play when you click a card, deal a card, or fold a stack (assuming your computer system is set up with a sound card and speakers).

6. When you finish playing, click the Close button.

 Stuck for a move? Try choosing Game➪Show An Available Move. If no move exists, you hear an annoying beeping sound. If one does exist, you hear angelic, harp-like music playing; then a lower-numbered card is highlighted, followed by the higher-numbered card that you should move it onto. Another way to show an available move is by clicking the score box near the bottom of the window or by pressing M.

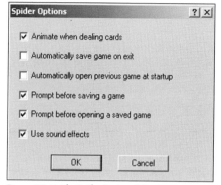

Figure 16-7: The Spider Options dialog box

Play Minesweeper

1. Choose Start➪All Programs➪Games➪Minesweeper to open the Minesweeper game board (see Figure 16-8).

2. Click a square on the board, and a timer starts counting the seconds of your game.

3. Continue to click squares on your game board. You can do the following three things:

   • If you click a square and a number appears, the number tells you how many mines are within the eight squares surrounding that square.

   • If you click a square and it remains blank, it tells you there are no mines within the eight squares surrounding it.

   • If you click a square and a bomb appears, all the hidden bombs are exposed (see Figure 16-9), and the game is over.

   • Right-click a square once to place a flag on it marking it as a mine. This causes the mine counter to count down. Now you can't set off this mine by clicking the square.

   • Right-click a square twice to place a question mark on it if you think it might contain a bomb to warn yourself to stay away for now.

Figure 16-8: A Minesweeper game in progress

Figure 16-9: The Minesweeper game board. I lost!

4. To begin a new game, choose Game⇨New. (Figure 16-10 shows a new game.) If you want to play a game with the same settings as the previous one you can simply click the smiley or frowny face icon.

5. You can set several game options through the Game menu (see Figure 16-11):

   • To change the expertise required, choose Game, and then choose Beginner, Intermediate, or Advanced.

   • To change the color of the playing board, choose Game⇨Color.

   • If you're a real sucker for pain, choose Game⇨Sound to have a loud dinging sound count off the seconds along with the timer, and send out a loud crashing noise if you uncover a bomb.

6. To end the game, click the Close button.

 If you want a bigger game board (more squares, more bombs, more fun), choose Game⇨Custom and specify the number of squares across, down, and the number of bombs hidden within them.

Figure 16-10: A new game

Figure 16-11: The Minesweeper Game menu

Play Internet Games

1. Choose Start➪All Programs➪Games, and then select one of these games: Internet Backgammon, Internet Checkers, Internet Hearts, Internet Reversi, or Internet Spades.

    I don't go into the rules for playing all these games, but you can click the Help button on this screen if you'd like to find out all about them.

2. In the resulting dialog box (Figure 16-12 shows an example), click Play to begin a game.

3. After being connected to the Zone.com game server, you're matched with an opponent and the board for the game that you selected appears.

4. Click the On setting of the chat feature and choose phrases, such as "It's your turn" or "Nice try," from the Chat drop-down list.

5. When you see that it's your turn (see Figure 16-13), make a move by clicking and dragging a game piece in some fashion, depending on the game you're playing.

    The game service matches you with another player by matching your primary language and skill level. Your skill level starts at Beginner, but as when you enter a game you can choose Game➪Skill Level and change that setting.

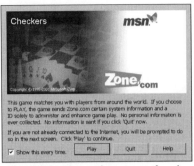

Figure 16-12: The introductory screen for online games at Zone.com

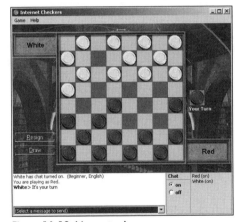

Figure 16-13: It's your turn!

Play Hearts

1. Choose Start⇨All Programs⇨Games⇨Hearts. In the resulting Microsoft Hearts Network dialog box, enter your name and click OK.

2. In the resulting Hearts window, shown in Figure 16-14, the player who has the two of clubs begins play by clicking three cards to pass to her opponent, and then clicking the Pass Left button.

3. Each player moving clockwise around the window plays a card of the same suit by clicking it. The one who plays the highest card of the suit in play wins the trick. (A trick is the cards you collect when you play the highest card of the suit.)

4. Choose Game⇨Options, to change the settings shown in Figure 16-15.

5. To end the game, choose Game⇨Exit or click the Close button.

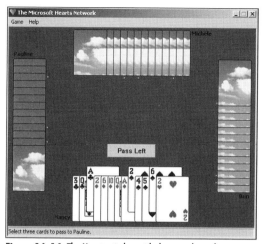

Figure 16-14: The Hearts window with three cards ready to be passed

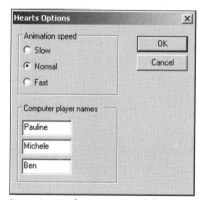

Figure 16-15: The Hearts Options dialog box

Add a USB Joystick to Your Computer

1. To connect a USB joystick or other type of game controller, simply plug it into a USB port on your computer. Connect to a game port by plugging the device into the port you want to use on your computer. Windows should recognize it and install it automatically.

2. If your device isn't recognized automatically, continue with the following steps.

3. Choose Start⇨Control Panel and double-click the Game Controllers icon.

4. In the resulting Game Controllers dialog box, shown in Figure 16-16, click Add.

5. In the resulting list of controllers (see Figure 16-17), click the one that you plugged in and then click OK twice.

 If your device controller isn't listed in the Game Controller dialog box, insert the installation disk that came with it and follow directions to install it. If you don't have an installation disk, either the device manual or the manufacturer's Web site might indicate that there's a compatible driver that's already installed with Windows that you could use, so follow Step 3 to select that driver. Alternatively, you can click the Custom button, make selections there, and Windows selects a likely driver. One final option: The manufacturer might offer a downloadable version of the driver on its Web site.

Figure 16-16: The Game Controllers dialog box

Figure 16-17: The list of available game controllers

Playing Music in Windows

*W*ho doesn't love music? It sets our toes tapping and puts a song in our hearts. It's the perfect accompaniment to spice up the drudgery of working on a computer for hours on end, so wouldn't it be great if you could play music right at your desk without having to take up valuable desktop space with a CD player?

Good news: You might not realize it, but your Windows XP computer is a lean, mean, music machine. With a sound card installed and speakers attached, it's a hi-tech desktop boombox that can play sound files and CDs. Using Windows media programs, you can create playlists and even listen to your favorite radio station while working or playing on your desktop or laptop computer.

The ins and outs of music on your computer, which you discover in this chapter, include

➡ Working with Windows Media Player and setting up a cool on-screen interface (called a skin) for it.

➡ Getting your computer ready for listening by setting up your speakers and adjusting the volume.

➡ Downloading music from the Internet or a CD and playing it.

➡ Managing your music by creating playlists of tracks you download, and even setting up your computer to play your favorite radio stations.

Chapter 17

Get ready to . . .

Choose a Skin for Windows Media Player

1. Connect to the Internet.

 Flip to Chapter 5 to find more information on Internet Explorer.

2. Choose Start⇨All Programs⇨Accessories⇨Entertainment⇨ Windows Media Player to open the Media Player, shown in Figure 17-1.

3. Click the Skin Chooser button, and then click the More Skins button to open the Windows Media page and choose a skin (an interface with neat graphics and colors).

4. Click any skin to download it and view the preview.

5. Click the Apply Skin button. The new skin is applied, looking cool and radical like the one shown in Figure 17-2.

 You can find out how to use the tools displayed on any Media Player skin in the "Play Music" task, later in this chapter. To return to the standard Media Player appearance, click the Return to Full Mode button located on every skin.

 Whole Web sites are devoted to skins for Media Player, such as The Skins Factory (www.theskinsfactory.com) and Skinz.org. Links to some of these are provided on the Windows Media page at www.microsoft.com/windows/ windowsmedia/9Series/GettingStarted/ Personalization/Skins.asp. Most skins that you find online are free for the taking, but check the terms of each site to be sure that a small fee isn't requested.

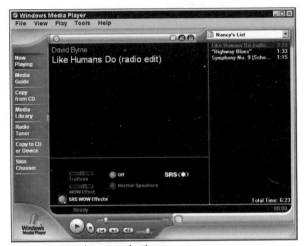

Figure 17-1: Windows XP Media Player

Figure 17-2: A new skin applied to Windows Media Player

Set Up Speakers

1. Attach speakers to your computer by plugging them into the appropriate connection (often labeled with a little megaphone or speaker symbol) on your CPU, laptop, or monitor.

2. Choose Start⇨Control Panel⇨Sounds and Audio Devices.

3. In the resulting Sounds and Audio Devices Properties dialog box (see Figure 17-3) click the Volume tab, and under Speaker Settings, click the Advanced button. (*Note:* The Volume tab should be selected by default; if it's not, click to display it.)

4. In the resulting Advanced Audio Properties dialog box, shown in Figure 17-4, use the Speaker Setup drop-down list to select the best option for your computer, and then click Apply.

5. Click the Performance tab of the Advanced Audio Properties dialog box to display it. Click either of two sliders shown here to modify these settings:

    *   **Hardware acceleration:** A higher setting can help your CPU by taking some sound processing chores off its plate. Changing this setting might help with some typical glitches that can occur. (The glitches mostly occur when using games, which drain your system resources to deal with high quality graphics and sound playback at the same time.)

    *   **Sample rate conversion quality:** A setting for sound quality. If you're experiencing problems with audio crashing your system or slowing your system's performance, putting this at a lower setting can help.

6. Click OK to save the new settings.

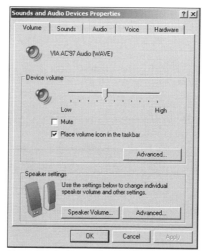

Figure 17-3: The Sounds and Audio Devices Properties dialog box

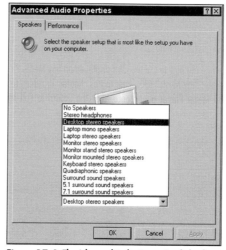

Figure 17-4: The Advanced Audio Properties dialog box

Adjust Volume

1. Choose Start⇨Control Panel⇨Sounds and Audio Devices to display the Sounds and Audio Devices Properties dialog box. Then select the Volume tab (shown in Figure 17-5) if it's not already displayed.

2. Under the Device Volume section, click the Advanced button to open the Volume Control dialog box, shown in Figure 17-6. Make any of the following settings:

   • Move the Volume sliders to adjust the volume up and down.

   • If you have a stereo device, use the Balance slider to adjust sound between right and left speakers.

   • To mute all devices or the selected device, select the Mute All or Mute check box underneath the specific device, respectively.

3. Click the Close button, and then click OK to close the Sounds and Audio Devices Properties dialog box.

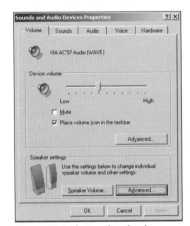

Figure 17-5: The Sounds and Audio Devices Properties dialog box, Volume tab

 The main Volume control works for all sound devices. If you have other devices installed (for example, a synthesizer or CD player), you can use individual sliders to adjust their volumes individually.

 A handy shortcut exists for quickly adjusting the volume (up or down) of your default sound devices. Click the Volume button (which looks like a little gray speaker) on the right side of the Windows taskbar. Use the slider on the Volume pop-up that appears to adjust the volume, or select the Mute check box to turn sounds off temporarily.

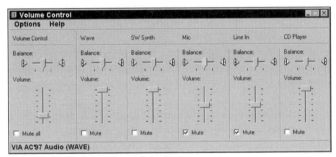

Figure 17-6: The Volume Control dialog box

Download a Sound File

1. Depending on how the Web site you're visiting has set things up, you do one of the following:

   - Click a download button or link and follow the instructions for selecting a destination location on your hard drive to download the file to.

   - Right-click the sound file link and choose Save Target As. In the Save As dialog box that appears, use the Save In drop-down list to locate a place to save the file, enter a File Name, and click Save. A dialog box (see Figure 17-7) shows the download progress; when it's completed, click the Open button. A player which the sound file is set up to use, such as MusicMatch Jukebox or Windows Media Player, will open and play the file.

   - Click the sound file link, and a download dialog box opens. Follow the steps in the preceding bullet to select a download location, name the file, and proceed with the download.

2. When the file finishes downloading, it might open and play automatically in a media player such as Windows Media Player, as shown in Figure 17-8. If it doesn't, you have to do one of the following actions:

   - Locate the saved file by using Windows Explorer, and double-click it to play it.

   - Open Windows Media Player, choose File⇨Open, locate the file, and open it. Then use the player's tools to play the file.

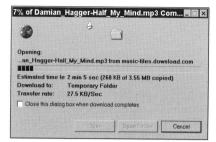

Figure 17-7: A file download in progress

 If you have installed Windows Service Pack 2 on your computer, it might block some downloads. You can use settings in Internet Explorer to control how downloads are handled. See Chapter 12 for more about SP2.

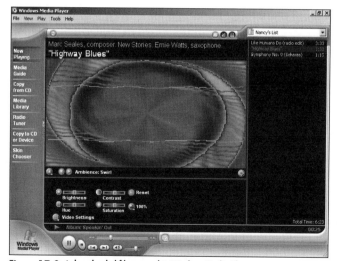

Figure 17-8: A downloaded file opened in Windows Media Player

Create a Playlist

1. Choose Start➪All Programs➪Accessories➪Entertainment➪ Windows Media Player.

2. Click the Media Library item, and then click Playlist button and select New Playlist. Enter the Playlist name and click OK.

3. Click a track in the left pane of the Media Library and it appears in the right pane (see Figure 17-9). Click the title listed on the right, and then click the Add to Playlist button, and click the playlist that you want to add it to in the menu that appears.

4. Under My Playlists in the left pane, click a playlist. All titles in the playlist appear in the list on the right (see Figure 17-10). Now you can do a few different things to manage the playlist. Click a title to select it, and then follow any of these steps:

    *   Click the Delete button to remove the title from the playlist.

    *   Click the Move Up button to move it higher in the playlist.

    *   Click the Move Down button to move it further down in the playlist.

    *   Click on Media Details button. If you're connected to the Internet, the Album Information pane appears, providing information about the track and artist.

5. To play a playlist, double-click it.

 You can rename or delete a playlist. Right-click the list under the My Playlists category in the left pane of the Media Library, and then choose Rename or Delete.

Figure 17-9: Titles listed in the Media Library

Figure 17-10: A playlist displayed in the Media Library

Copy Music to a CD

1. Insert a blank CD suitable for storing audio files in your computer CD-RW drive.

2. Open the Windows Media Player, click the Media Library button, and then click an album or playlist to open it.

3. Click the Copy to CD or Device button on the left side of the player. The titles on the currently open item appear in the left pane, and a Music on Device pane appears to the right (see Figure 17-11).

4. Select the check box next to a title, and then click the Copy Music button. The music is copied onto the CD.

 Want to copy music from a CD into your Windows Media Player Library? Just put the CD in your computer drive and click the Copy from CD button on the left. When the list of titles on the CD appears, click to select the ones you want, and then click the Copy Music button in the top-right corner.

 When you copy music to a CD, you create an exact copy, but if you copy music from a CD onto your computer, Windows Media Player automatically compresses it. That's because music files are big and can fill up your hard drive fast. Compressed music files lose some sound quality, but given the quality of your computer speakers, when you play music from your computer, you probably won't notice the difference.

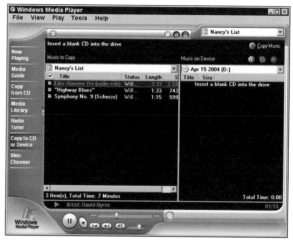

Figure 17-11: Copy music to a CD

 If you're swapping music online through various music sharing services, then copying them to CD and passing them around to your friends, always do a virus check on the files before handing them off. Also, be sure you have the legal right to download and swap music with others.

Play Music

1. Choose Start➪All Programs➪Accessories➪Entertainment➪ Windows Media Player.

2. Click the Media Library button on the left to display the library shown in Figure 17-12. Click an album or playlist to open it; the titles of the songs are displayed in the right pane.

3. Use the buttons here to do the following:

   • Click a track, and then click the Play button to play it.

   • Click the Stop button to stop playback.

   • Click the Next or Previous buttons to move to the next or previous track in an album or playlist.

   • Use the Mute and Volume controls to pump the sound up or down without having to modify the Windows volume settings.

    Use the Quick Access drop-down list box in the top right area of the Windows Media Player. (In Figure 17-2, this box displays Nancy's List.) Click the arrow to quickly select a playlist.

Figure 17-12: The Media Library

 Note that different skins display controls that have a different look. However, all is not lost. Until you get used to the new controls, just hover your mouse over each control and a ToolTip appears telling you which is which.

Listen to the Radio

1. Double-click the Internet Explorer icon on the Windows desktop to open the browser.

2. Choose View⇨Explorer Bar⇨Media.

3. In the resulting WindowsMedia.com pane, click a featured radio station, or click the More Radio Stations link to display a screen like the one shown in Figure 17-13.

4. Click a Category of music. (Alternatively, you can click a link under the Editor's Pick heading or click a Listen Now link for one of the featured stations to go directly to a station).

5. Click the link (which might be labeled Go Listen, Website, or just be the name of the station) for one of the stations.

6. In the site that opens in a separate window, use the various tools and features on that site to control the music that's played there:

   - To listen to another station, close the window of the station that you selected and click another category or another station link.

   - To search for a station, enter a keyword in the Search text box and click the Search button.

   - To display a comprehensive radio guide, click the arrow on the Media Options button at the bottom of the Media pane on the left and choose Radio Guide (shown in Figure 17-14).

   - Click an item in the Radio Guide to display more information, and then click one of two links: Add to My Stations or Visit Website to Play. If you add the item to My Stations, it is listed in the My Stations of Windows Media Player's radio feature so that you can play it with a single click.

Figure 17-13: A variety of radio stations to choose from

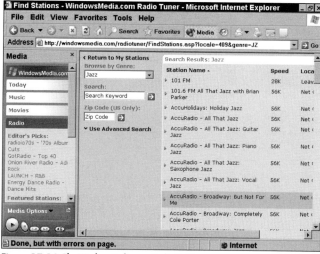

Figure 17-14: The WindowsMedia.com Radio Guide

Editing Movies in Windows

First camcorders, which have become as ubiquitous as flowers in spring, made Hollywood directors of the average person on the street. Now computers and video software provide people who own Windows with the tools to play and edit movies to their hearts' content. Microsoft has built two such tools into Windows Movie Maker for editing and organizing movies, and Media Player to play movies.

So where do these movies come from? A sample movie clip is included with Windows in the My Videos folder to get you started. You can also upload video files from your camcorder, or if you're one of the few folks who don't actually own a camcorder, you can download movies from the Internet or get your friends who have camcorders to save their movies as electronic files and e-mail them to you.

When you have movies to play with, here's what you can do:

➠ Play back your movies using features to play, pause, stop, fast forward or rewind.

➠ Open movies in Movie Maker, build a storyboard to organize the frames in any order you wish, and modify the timeline for individual clips. (This trimming of clips is what's known in the movie biz as editing.)

➠ Record a narration that is saved right along with your movie file.

Get ready to . . .

Play Movies with Windows Media Player

1. Choose Start➪All Programs➪Accessories➪Entertainment➪ Windows Media Player.

2. In the resulting Media Player window, choose File➪ Open to display the Open dialog box.

3. Use the Look In drop-down list to locate the folder that contains the file you want to play. Click the file, and then click Open.

4. The movie opens in the Media Player. Choose View➪ Now Playing Tools➪Video Settings.

5. Click and drag any of the following sliders (see Figure 18-1) to adjust the settings:

   - **Brightness:** How light or dark the image is.

   - **Contrast:** The variation between dark and light colors.

   - **Hue:** Relates to where a color falls on the color spectrum (green to blue, for example).

   - **Saturation:** How pure a color's hue is, from gray to pure color.

6. Click the Play button to begin the playback (see Figure 18-2). Adjust the volume of any sound track by using the Mute or Volume tools.

 To stop the movie before it finishes, click the Stop button. Note that the Previous and Next tools aren't available for single movie clips — they jump you from one track to another when playing sound files.

7. Click the Close button to close the Media Player.

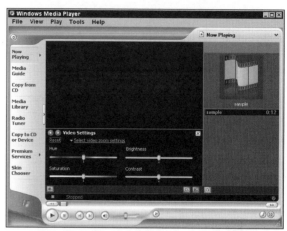

Figure 18-1: The Windows Media Player with a movie clip opened

Figure 18-2: A movie in playback mode

Create a New Project in Windows Movie Maker

1. Choose Start⇨All Programs⇨Accessories⇨Windows Movie Maker to open the Movie Maker window.

2. Choose File⇨New⇨Project to open a new blank Movie Maker file, and then save the file.

3. Choose File⇨Import to open the Select the File to Import dialog box.

4. Use the Look In drop-down list to locate the folder where the movie file you want to open is saved.

5. Click the file, and then click Open to open the file in the Movie Maker window, as shown in Figure 18-3. (*Note:* You can repeat this procedure to open more than one movie file in a project.)

6. Choose File⇨Save Project. In the Save Project dialog box shown in Figure 18-4, enter a filename in the File Name text box, and then click Save.

 Now that you've created a project, what can you actually do with it? When you've created a project and imported movies into it, you can use various features of Movie Maker to edit, reorganize, and play-back movies. These features are covered later in this chapter. With more than one movie imported into a project, for example, you could pick and choose clips from each of them and organize them to create your own unique movie.

 Another nice feature when playing back movies in Windows Movie Maker is the ability to view movies with the full screen by clicking the Full Screen button. Press Escape to exit Full Screen mode.

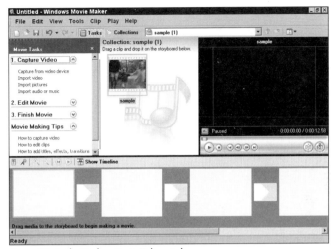

Figure 18-3: The Windows Movie Maker window

Figure 18-4: The Save Project dialog box

Organize Clips in a Storyboard

1. Open a project in Movie Maker. If the Storyboard isn't displayed at the bottom of the screen, click the Show Storyboard button.

2. In the Collections pane, click the collection that the clip you want to work with belongs to display the collection in the workspace.

3. Click a movie clip and drag it to a box on the Storyboard, shown in Figure 18-5. To manage clips on the Storyboard, perform any of these actions:

   - **Insert a clip between adjacent clips:** Click a clip and drag so that your mouse cursor rests on the line between the adjacent clips. Release your mouse.

   - **Reorganize clips:** Click and drag clips that you've already placed on the Storyboard to new locations.

   - **Remove a clip:** Right-click it and choose Cut from the shortcut menu, as shown in Figure 18-6. The remaining clips to the right move over to fill in the blank space on the Storyboard. Note that you can use the scroll bar at the bottom of the Storyboard to move from left to right to view all clips placed on it.

   - **Copy a clip:** On either the Storyboard or the workspace, right-click it and choose Copy. Then choose Edit⇨Paste to paste a copy at the end of the list of clips in the workspace or in the first blank space on the right of the Storyboard.

4. When you finish editing your storyboard, be sure to save it by choosing File⇨Save Project. It's saved with the .mswmm file extension.

Figure 18-5: Movie frames placed on the Storyboard

To playback an entire storyboard, choose Play⇨Play Entire Storyboard/Timeline. Each clip is highlighted on the Storyboard as it plays.

Figure 18-6: The shortcut menu for Storyboard clips

Edit a Movie Timeline

1. With Windows Movie Maker displayed and a project open on the Storyboard, choose View⇨Timeline.

2. Use the Timeline that appears at the bottom of the screen to help guide you in making cuts to clips to modify their lengths using these features:

   • Choose Play⇨Play Clip to begin playback, and then choose Play⇨Pause Clip. Click a clip on the Storyboard at the point where you want to begin the cut, and then choose Clip⇨Set Start Trim Point.

   • When the movie gets to the point where you want to end the edit, choose Clip⇨Set End Trim Point (see Figure 18-7).

3. To add a transition between clips (that is a cross-fade effect that makes one clip seem to dissolve into another) click the edge of one clip on the Storyboard and drag to the left or right to create an overlap between clips (see Figure 18-8). This overlap creates the transition.

4. To split a clip into two portions you can move around in the storyboard separately, select the video clip that you want to split in the Collections pane. Choose Play⇨ Play/Pause. Choose Clip⇨Split. The clip is now split, with a number (2) added to the name of the second portion.

5. When you're done editing, don't forget to save the project (File⇨Save Project).

 If you want to join several clips that are next to each other on the Storyboard into one clip, press and hold Shift, and then click the first and last clips. Choose Clip⇨Combine. You can also select noncontiguous clips by holding down Ctrl while you select clips.

Figure 18-7: Editing a movie by using the Timeline

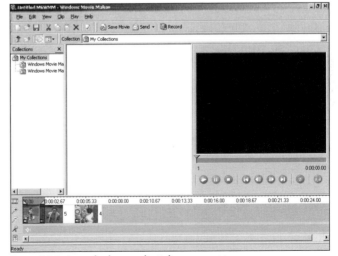

Figure 18-8: An overlap between clips indicates a transition

Record a Narration

1. With a project open in Windows Movie Maker, choose Tools⇨Narrate Timeline.

2. In the resulting Narrate Timeline dialog box (see Figure 18-9) click the Record Level slider and drag it up or down to increase or decrease the record volume level.

 Windows sets you up with your default computer microphone and recording device, so unless you've got a sound studio set up in your basement, you're probably safe leaving this at its default setting.

 If the movie clip already contains audio, you have to select the Mute Video Soundtrack check box to avoid conflict between your recorded narration and the existing track.

3. Click the Start Narration button, and the video begins to play. Begin speaking into your computer microphone. When you're done, click the Stop Narration button. If you've finished recording narrations for this movie, click the Done link.

4. In the resulting Save Windows Media File dialog box, shown in Figure 18-10, locate a folder to save the file in by using the Save In drop-down list.

 Have you said something worth repeating? You can save narrations to various points in your movie by clicking and dragging the narration file onto the Storyboard.

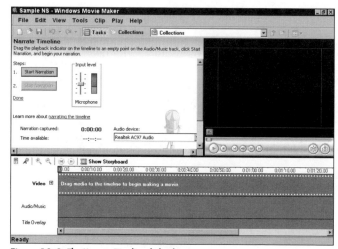

Figure 18-9: The Narrate Timeline dialog box

Figure 18-10: The Save Windows Media File dialog box

Add a Title or Credit

1. With Windows Movie Maker open and a clip displayed, choose Tools⇨Titles and Credits.

2. In the pane that appears in the upper-left corner (see Figure 18-11), click the appropriate link to add a title or credit in a desired location.

3. In the Enter Title Text window that appears, type the text for the title or credit.

4. To change the font effects on the text you entered, scroll down in the window and click the Change the Title Text Font and Color link.

5. In the Select Font and Color window do any of the following:

   - Use the font drop down list to select a different font.

   - Click on the color button to display a palette of text colors; click on a color, then on OK to apply it.

   - Click and drag the slider for the Transparency setting to make the text more transparent.

   - Click the Increase Text Size or Decrease Text Size buttons to change the size.

   - Click on the Align Text Right, Center Text, or Align Text Left buttons to change the alignment on the video clip.

   - Click the Bold, Italic, or Underlined buttons to apply those effects.

6. When you've finished making settings, click the Done, Add to Movie link and the credit or title appears in the Timeline (see Figure 18-12).

 You can click the Change Title Animation link when in the Title and Credits window to have your title or credit explode on screen, fly in from one side, or spin and zoom around your screen, for example.

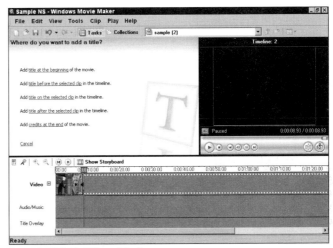

Figure 18-11: The Titles and Credits pane

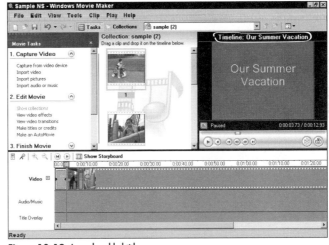

Figure 18-12: A newly added title

Add Video Effects

1. With a movie open in Movie Maker, choose Tools⇨ Video Effects.

2. In the Video Effects pane shown in Figure 18-13, click on an effect and drag it to a clip in your movie on the Storyboard or timeline. A star appears on a clip to indicate it has an effect applied.

3. To add several affects to a selected clip at once, choose Clip⇨Video⇨Video Effects.

4. In the Add or Remove Video Effects dialog box shown in Figure 18-14, click on any effect in the list on the left, and then click Add. To remove an effect click on any effect in the list on the right and click Remove.

5. When you're finished click the OK button. When you click the Play button to play the video, you can view your stunning effects.

 Note that some of the effects are available only if you purchase Microsoft Plus! If you select one of those effects a window will pop up, informing you of this and providing a link to a Web site where you can purchase this software. Microsoft Plus! includes various media enhancing tools and clips.

Figure 18-13: The Video Effects pane

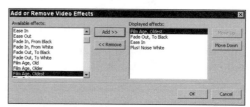

Figure 18-14: The Add or Remove Video Effects dialog box

Part VII
Practical Applications

Working Remotely

We live in a hurry-up-and-go society. Gone are the days when you could sit back during your flight from Des Moines to Chicago and take a snooze. These days, people do as much work in the air and on the road as in cubicles and offices.

Windows XP hasn't left the road warrior behind: It offers several features that help keep you in touch and help you connect your Windows computer to mobile devices, such as a personal digital assistant (PDA) or cell phone.

The Windows XP remote control features include:

➠ Power management tools for laptops to make sure that you don't run out of juice at an all-important moment.

➠ A way to connect infrared-enabled devices to your computer to transfer data between them.

➠ A feature that lets you send documents on your computer over a phone line to a fax machine.

➠ Features to let your modem dial from a remote location by setting up a different originating location than your home or office, and even dial by using a calling card for long distance calls.

Chapter
19

Get ready to . . .

Set Power Management Options for a Laptop

1. Choose Start⇨Control Panel, click the Performance and Maintenance link, and then click the Power Options Control Panel icon.

2. In the Power Options Properties dialog box on the Power Schemes tab shown in Figure 19-1, use the Power Schemes drop-down list to select the Portable/Laptop option.

3. In the specific settings that appear for the Portable/Laptop option (see Figure 19-2), make selections from the four drop-down lists to manage the length of time for certain features, such as how long the monitor waits to turns off when not in use and when the system goes into a standby mode.

4. Click OK to save your laptop power settings.

 The Hibernate setting, which you enable and disable on the Hibernate tab of the Power Options Properties dialog box, is a feature that allows you to turn off your computer, but when you turn it on again, you return to wherever you were. So, for example, instead of coming up with the Windows desktop, you see the game of Minesweeper that you were playing, and it's all ready to pick up where you left off. This saves battery power and time on trips where work is often interrupted.

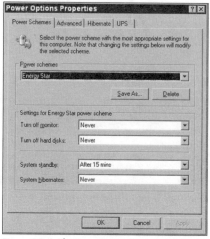

Figure 19-1: The Power Options Properties dialog box

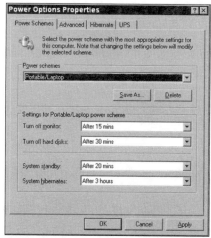

Figure 19-2: The Portable/Laptop options

Set Up a Low Battery Warning for a Laptop

1. Choose Start⇨Control Panel, click the Performance and Maintenance link, and then click the Power Options Control Panel icon.

2. In the Power Options Properties dialog box, click the Alarms tab (see Figure 19-3).

3. On the Alarms tab, use the sliders in the Low Battery Alarm and Critical Battery Alarm items to set them to go off at the level you prefer.

4. Click the Alarm Action radio button and select the setting that you prefer. For example, when the alarm goes off, you might want the computer to shut down.

5. Click OK to save the new settings.

 Windows XP should discern any power options your specific device offers, so some settings might vary slightly depending on your setup and machine.

 The best defense is a good offense. That's why a true road warrior defends against losing battery power by carrying a spare, fully charged battery. When you get a warning that you're running low, shut things down, remove the depleted culprit, and slip in the new battery. Then go on your merry way!

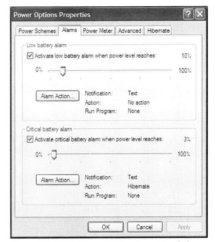

Figure 19-3: The Power Options Properties dialog box, Alarms tab

 You can set a low battery alarm, a critical battery alarm, or both. Typically, a low battery alarm gives you a good amount of warning — say, when you're at 25 percent of battery capacity. The critical alarm is the "look out, your laptop is about to go into a coma at any minute" type of warning.

Connect Infrared-Enabled Devices

1. Choose Start⇨My Network Places, and then click the View Network Connections link.

2. In the Network Connections window, click the Create a New Connection link.

3. In the New Connection Wizard, click Next.

4. In the Network Connection Type window, select the Set Up an Advanced Connection radio button (see Figure 19-4), and click Next.

5. In the Advanced Connection Options window, select the Connect Directly to Another Computer radio button, and click Next.

6. In the Host or Guest window (see Figure 19-5), select Host if you have information on your computer to send to the device or Guest if you want to download information from the device and click Next.

7. Your next move depends on your selection in Step 6. If you selected Guest in Step 6, you must enter a name in the Connection Name text box, and then click Next. (If you selected Host in Step 6, this step isn't necessary.) Use the Device for This Connection drop-down list to select the Infrared Port option.

8. Click Next.

9. In the Connection Name window, if you specified Host, under User Permissions use the Name box to enter information about the users who can connect. If you specified Guest, under Connection Availability you can select the Anyone's Use or My Use Only option.

10. Click Next to make the connection.

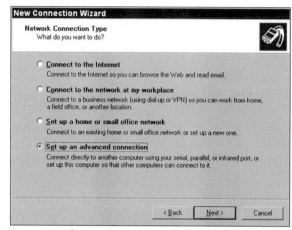

Figure 19-4: The Network Connection window

 You might have to reboot your computer to have this connection take effect. If so, you will see a message from Windows instructing you to do so.

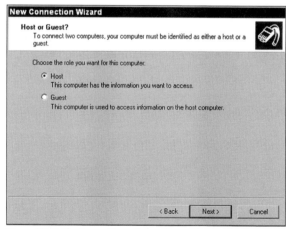

Figure 19-5: The Host or Guest window

Fax a Cover Memo from Your Computer

1. Choose Start➪All Programs➪Accessories➪
    Communications➪Fax➪Fax Console.

2. If you haven't set up the Fax feature, the Fax Configuration
    Wizard appears. Click Next and enter information in the
    second wizard window, as shown in Figure 19-6. Click
    Next again, and then in the resulting window, click Finish.

3. In the resulting Fax Console window, to send a fax cover
    page, choose File➪Send a Fax.

4. In the Send Fax Wizard, click Next. In Recipient
    Information window, shown in Figure 19-7, enter the
    recipient's information and click Next.

5. In the Preparing the Cover Page window that appears,
    select a style from the Cover Page Template drop-down
    list. Fill in the Subject Line text box and type your mes-
    sage in the Note text box. Click Next.

6. In the Schedule window, select a radio button to specify
    when to send the fax (Now, When Discount Rates
    Apply, or a Specific Time Within the Next 24 Hours)
    and to set a Priority, if you want to. Click Next.

7. In the Completing the Send Fax Wizard window, click
    Preview Fax to see what it will look like.

8. Click the Close button to close the preview, and then
    click Finish to send the fax. A Fax Monitor window
    appears, showing you the progress of the fax.

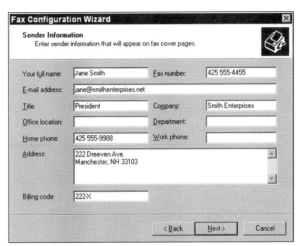

Figure 19-6: The Fax Configuration Wizard

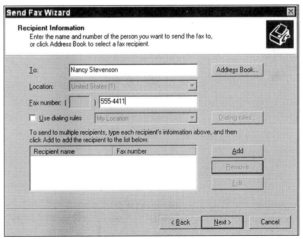

Figure 19-7: The Send Fax Wizard

Send a Document as a Fax

1. With the document open in an application, such as Word or Excel, choose File➪Print.

2. In the Print dialog box (see Figure 19-8), click the arrow on the Printer Name drop-down list to display it and select Fax.

3. In the Welcome to Send Fax Wizard window that appears, click Next.

4. In the Send Fax Wizard window, enter the recipient's information and click Next.

5. In the Preparing the Cover Page window, shown in Figure 19-9, select a style from the Cover Page Template drop-down list. Fill in the Subject Line text box and type your message in the Note text box. Click Next.

6. In the Schedule window, select a radio button to specify when to send the fax (Now, When Discount Rates Apply, or a Specific Time Within the Next 24 Hours), and to set a Priority, if you want to. Click Next.

7. In the Completing the Send Fax Wizard window, click Preview Fax to see what it will look like.

8. Click the Close button to close the preview, and then click Finish to send the fax. A Fax Monitor window appears, showing you the progress of the fax.

 The Fax Console might not have installed with Windows. If you can't find the feature, go to the Control Panel and click the Add or Remove Programs link. Click the Add/Remove Windows Components button and select the Fax Services option in the Components list. Follow the instructions to install it.

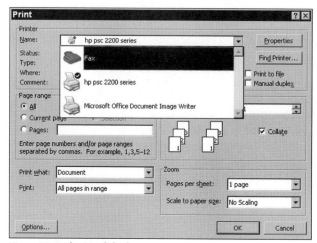

Figure 19-8: The Print dialog box

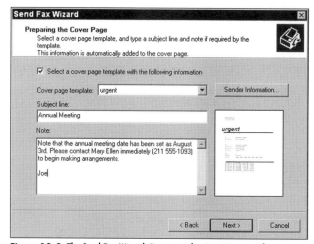

Figure 19-9: The Send Fax Wizard, Preparing the Cover Page window

Set Up Long Distance Dialing Away from Home

1. Choose Start⇨Control Panel, click the Printers and Other Hardware link, and then the Phone and Modem Options link.

2. In the Phone and Modem Options dialog box, shown in Figure 19-10, click an item in the Location list box, and then click the New button.

3. In the New Location dialog box, shown in Figure 19-11, enter a name in the Location Name text box.

4. Select the country to call from in the Country/Region drop-down list, and enter the area code to call from in the Area Code text box.

5. Set the following options:

   • If you're required to enter numbers to access an outside or long distance line, enter that information in the appropriate text box in the Dialing Rules area.

   • If you use a call waiting feature and want to disable it for this dialing location, select the To Disable Call Waiting, Dial check box and enter the code used to disable the feature for your phone service.

 If you want to set up a location to use a prefix (for example, a country code) before an area code, display the Area Code Rules tab of the New Location dialog box and create a new Area Code Rule.

 If you have more esoteric dialing needs, check out the Advanced tab of the Phone and Modem Options dialog box (see Figure 19-11). Here you find TAPI (Telephony Application Programming Interface) providers for setting up a Windows application to access your server's voice service. People often use these kinds of connections for multicast conferencing. If you don't know what that is, you'll probably never need this setting.

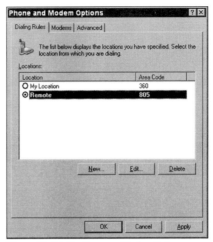

Figure 19-10: The Phone and Modem Options dialog box

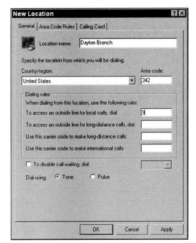

Figure 19-11: The New Location dialog box

Set Up a Calling Card

1. Choose Start⇨Control Panel, click the Printers and Other Hardware link, and then click the Phone and Modem Options link.

2. In the Phone and Modem Options dialog box, shown in Figure 19-12, select an option from the Location list box, and then click the Edit button.

3. In the Edit Location dialog box, click the Calling Card tab (shown in Figure 19-13).

4. Select an option in the Card Types list box.

5. Enter the calling card number in the Account Number text box, and enter the PIN in the Personal ID Number text box.

6. Click OK to save the settings.

If you have a calling card that isn't listed in the Card Types list box on the Calling Card tab, leave the default setting of None, and then click the New button to enter information about your specific calling card.

If you have a problem when your modem dials a number, you might not be getting a dial tone before the dialing begins. On the Modems tab of the Phone and Modem Options dialog box, select the Wait for Dial Tone Before Dialing check box to solve this.

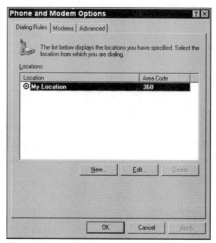

Figure 19-12: The Phone and Modem Options dialog box

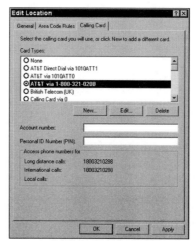

Figure 19-13: The Edit Location dialog box, Calling Card tab

Make a Dialup Connection by Using an Infrared-Enabled Cellular Phone

1. If necessary, check with your phone manufacturer or documentation to make sure that the infrared feature is turned on.

2. Line up the infrared transceiver on your phone and the transceiver on your computer within a couple feet of each other.

3. Choose Start➪My Network Places.

4. In the My Network Places window, click the View Network Connections link.

5. In the Network Connections window (shown in Figure 19-14), click the Create a New Connection link, and then click Next to proceed with the New Connection Wizard.

6. In the Network Connection Type window, shown in Figure 19-15, click any of the four connection types, depending on what kind of connection you want to set up.

7. Continue with the various wizard settings. When you finish the wizard, you should be able to connect to this location by using your cellular phone, as long as your phone and computer are aligned properly.

 If you're not sure whether your computer or laptop supports infrared connections, look for a small, dark red window on the computer or laptop case (that's the infrared transceiver; it looks like a similar box on your TV remote control), or check your device documentation. You can also go to the Device Manager through the Control Panel and look under Infrared Devices to see whether any are listed.

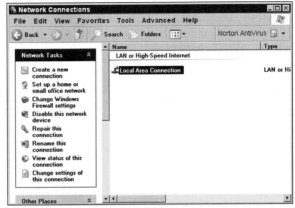

Figure 19-14: The Network Connections window

 For more about the specifics of using the New Connection Wizard to set up connections, see Chapter 4.

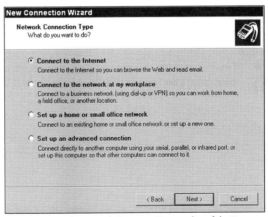

Figure 19-15: The Network Connection Type window of the New Connection Wizard

Working with Windows-Based Applications

*I*f you've used ATM cards at bank machines, you've probably noticed that they all work pretty much the same. From one bank's card to another's, and from machine to machine, some things differ, but mainly if you've used one, you know how to use them all.

In a similar way, software that runs in the Windows XP environment typically shares certain basic functionality. I grant that you might occasionally run into a hand-rolled, Mom-and-Pop software package that handles some of these functions a bit differently, but for just about any Windows XP-compatible software package that you buy from a mainstream software manufacturer, this common functionality applies.

You find menus, menu commands, and certain dialog boxes that are remarkably similar (for example Print, Open, and Save As) if not identical from one program to the next. Of course, programs from Microsoft are the most consistent with their Windows XP operating system.

So in this chapter, you discover some of these common functions of Windows-based software applications, which can give you a jump start with any program that you use. For all these tasks, you first open the application (which you can find out how to do in Chapter 1). I used Microsoft Word for the tasks in this chapter.

Chapter 20

Get ready to . . .

Open Files

1. Choose File⇨Open.

2. In the Open dialog box shown in Figure 20-1, select the location of the file from the Look In drop-down list or click an icon on the left side of the dialog box to view categories, such as My Documents, My Computer, or Desktop.

3. If necessary, double-click a folder in the list that appears to open it to show files contained within.

4. Select the file that you want to open, and then click the Open button.

 If you want to look only for files of a certain type, select that type in the Files of Type drop-down list in the Open dialog box. Doing so restricts the list to the types of files that the application can open.

 Need more information about a file to be sure that it's the one you want to open, such as the date you last saved it? Click the arrow on the View icon near the upper-right corner in the Open dialog box and select the Details view. This displays the filename, size, format, and date last modified.

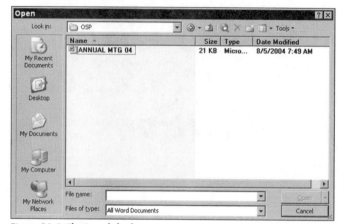

Figure 20-1: The Open dialog box

 Still can't find the file you want to open? With the Open dialog box displayed, click the Tools button and select Search. A File Search dialog box appears, putting both basic and advanced search tools at your fingertips.

Print Documents

1. Choose File⇨Print.

2. In the Print dialog box, shown in Figure 20-2, be sure that the printer you want to print to is displayed in the Printer area. If it's not, select it from the Name drop-down list.

3. In the Print Range area, select an option. These might vary depending on the application, but typically include

- **All:** To print the entire document.

- **Current Page:** To print the currently displayed page, slide, or spreadsheet, for example.

- **Pages:** To specify a range of pages, such as 3-6 for pages 3 through 6, or 3, 7, 9 to print pages 3, 7, and 9.

4. In the Copies area, click the spinner arrows to select the number of copies to print.

5. When you finish making selections, click OK.

 You might see a Print What drop-down list, which allows you to select the type of document to print. For example, in Word you can print the document, document styles, or document properties. In PowerPoint, you might print handouts, an outline, or slides.

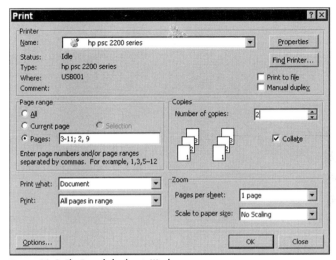

Figure 20-2: The Print dialog box in Word

 You might also see a Collate check box in the Print dialog box. If you're printing multiple copies, selecting this check box makes copies print in organized sets. (For example, with 4 copies you get 4 sets from page 1 to the end, rather than 4 page 1's followed by 4 page 2's, and so on.)

 The sizing feature, another fairly standard setting, might vary slightly from application to application. By using this feature, you can scale the printout to fit a certain number of printed pages, which typically reduces the size of larger documents to fit more on a page (but usually doesn't enlarge smaller documents to fill the page).

Save Files for the First Time

1. Choose File⇨Save.

2. In the Save As dialog box shown in Figure 20-3, locate the folder where you want to save the file by using the Save In drop-down list or by clicking an icon along the left side, such as My Documents or My Computer.

3. In the File Name text box, enter a descriptive name for the file.

4. If you want to save the file in a format other than the default application format, open the Save as Type drop-down list and select the format.

5. Click the Save button to save the file in the location and with the name you specified.

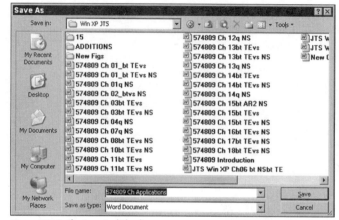

Figure 20-3: The Save As dialog box

 If you've saved a document before, choosing File⇨Save saves the most recent changes to the document without having to go through the Save As dialog box settings again. However, if you want to save an existing document with another name or different settings (such as a new format), select File⇨Save As and enter the new information. The newly saved file doesn't overwrite the original, but does create a new version.

 You might also look for a Save as Web Page command on many File menus. This allows you to publish a document in a format that will be readable by browsers if you post to a Web site.

 If you're saving a file and want to create a new folder to save it in, from within the Save As dialog box click the New Folder button, enter a folder name in the New Folder dialog box, click OK, and then proceed to enter a filename and click Save to save the file in the new folder.

Insert Objects

1. Choose Insert⇨Object.

2. In the resulting Object dialog box (see Figure 20-4), select an item in the Object Type list. Then do one of the following:

- Click OK to create a new object. If that's your choice, you're done. If not, move right along with this next step.

- Click the Create from File tab and then click the Browse button and continue following this list.

3. In the Browse dialog box (see Figure 20-5), find the location of the file by using the Look In drop-down list; select the file and then click the Insert button.

4. If you want to insert a link to the object rather than the object itself, select the Link to File check box.

5. Click OK.

 If you want to display the object as an icon that the user can click to display the item, rather than as an object itself, be sure to select the Display as Icon check box before closing the Insert Object dialog box. You can even use a different icon by clicking the Change Icon button in the Object dialog box, Create from File tab and locating a different image.

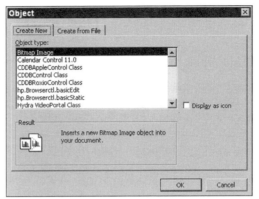

Figure 20-4: The Object dialog box

 You can also typically find other commands on the Insert menus of Windows applications to insert pictures, other files, or objects that you create in small applications provided with suites of software, such as Office.

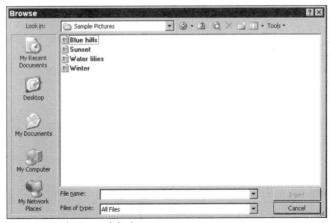

Figure 20-5: The Browse dialog box

Cut, Copy, and Paste

1. Click and drag across the text that you want to work with, or click an object to select it, as in Figure 20-6.

2. Choose Edit⇨Cut (see Figure 20-7) to remove the selected item from its present location and place it elsewhere, or choose Edit⇨Copy to make a copy of the item to place elsewhere.

3. Move your cursor to the location (in the current document, another document, or another application) where you want to place the item, and then choose Edit⇨Paste.

 Most applications also offer toolbar buttons for Cut, Copy, and Paste, as well as keyboard shortcuts. The common keyboard shortcuts are: Cut, Ctrl+X; Copy, Ctrl+C; and Paste, Ctrl+V.

 One slick feature of Microsoft applications is Paste Special (see Figure 20-7). This displays a smart tag icon when you paste an item. If you click this icon, you get some choices about whether you retain formatting from the original item or assume the formatting of the location where you're pasting it.

Figure 20-6: A selected picture

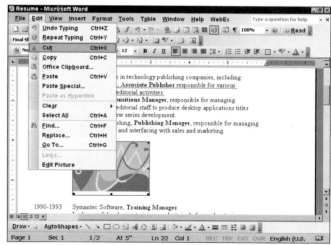

Figure 20-7: The Edit menu in Microsoft Word

Format Text

1. Click and drag to select the text that you want to format.

2. Choose Format⇨Font to display the Font dialog box (see Figure 20-8).

3. Adjust the following settings:

   - Select a font in the Font list box to apply a certain typeface style to the selected text, such as Arial or Times Roman.

   - Select a style in the Font Style list box to apply effects or combinations of effects, such as Bold Italic.

   - Select a size in the Size list box to apply a size to selected text, or type a number in the Size text box.

   - Select various check boxes in the Effects area, such as Underline, Shadow, or Emboss. *Note:* Not all applications allow all of these effects.

   - Click the arrow on the Font Color drop-down list to display a palette of colors (see Figure 20-9). Select a color to apply it to the text.

4. When you finish making settings, click OK to apply them.

 Many applications offer alternative ways to select text rather than clicking and dragging. For example, Word offers a selection bar feature along the left edge of the document. Place your cursor along the left side of the page and click to select an entire line at once. You can also double-click in the selection bar to select an entire paragraph, or triple-click to select all the text in the document.

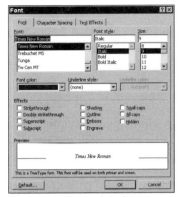

Figure 20-8: The Font dialog box

 Most Windows-based applications also offer toolbar buttons and drop-down lists to apply individual formatting effects, such as Font, Font Size, Bold, Italic, and Underline. To display a Formatting toolbar, typically you choose View⇨Toolbar, and then choose the toolbar that you want to display to place a check mark next to it.

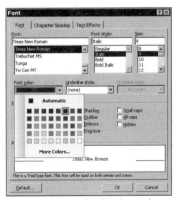

Figure 20-9: The Color drop-down palette

Insert a Hyperlink

1. Click in the document where you want to place the hyperlink.

2. Choose Insert⇨Hyperlink.

3. In the Insert Hyperlink dialog box (see Figure 20-10), select one of the categories of item to link to by clicking it in the Link To section on the left: An Existing File or Web Page; Place In This Document; Create New Document; or E-Mail Address.

4. Depending on what you select in Step 3, you see different options, such as the choices for the Place in This Document category, as shown in Figure 20-11.

5. Make choices or enter information appropriate for the place you want to insert a link to, and then enter the link text in the Text to Display box.

6. Click OK to insert the link (see Figure 20-12).

 You can insert a hyperlink on a line of a Word Perfect document, in a text box on a PowerPoint slide, or in a cell of a spreadsheet program, for example.

 If you want a ScreenTip to display when someone using the document hovers a mouse over the inserted link, click the ScreenTip button in the Insert Hyperlink dialog box and enter the text in the ScreenTip Text box and click OK.

Figure 20-10: The Insert Hyperlink dialog box

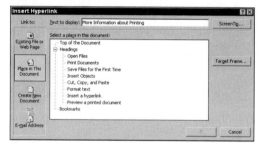

Figure 20-11: The Place in This Document options

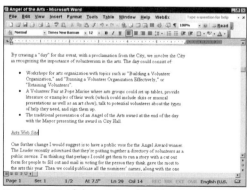

Figure 20-12: A link inserted in a Word document

Preview a Printed Document

1. Choose File⇨Print Preview.

2. In the Print Preview window, as shown in Figure 20-13, use various buttons on the toolbar to modify the view (for example, zooming in or out, or displaying two or more pages instead of one).

3. To print the document without changing any settings, click the Print button. To close the Print Preview window, click the Close button in the upper-right corner.

When you open a menu such as File in a Windows application, often only the most commonly used options are displayed. Print Preview might be one of those commands not immediately available to you. You can click the double-arrows at the bottom of the menu to display all choices or wait a few moments for the application to display all available commands.

Many Print Preview features allow you to simply click a previewed page to zoom in and click again to zoom out. A small magnifying glass icon usually tells you what the next click will do. If the icon has a plus symbol, it zooms in, and a minus symbol means that it zooms out.

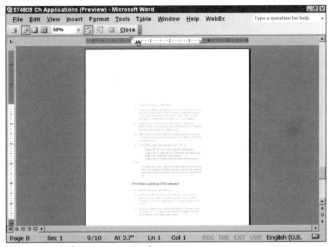

Figure 20-13: The Print Preview window

To change document settings, such as margin or layout, before printing it, you typically choose File⇨Page Setup. Some Print Previews offer a Page Setup button to take you to the document settings before printing.

Project: Organize Your Desktop

*I*n this project, you (finally!) get yourself organized by customizing the icons on the Windows desktop. The desktop is like a Windows control center that allows you to make applications easy to access:

➠ You can create desktop shortcuts that take you to frequently used programs, files, and folders.

➠ You can add or delete desktop shortcuts and rearrange them.

➠ You can use the Quick Launch bar (located on the taskbar along the bottom of the desktop) to stash your favorite programs for one-click access.

In this chapter, you get to work on organizing your own desktop by adding a shortcut to the Windows Calculator, adding your antivirus software to the Quick Launch bar, and generally organizing the way icons are arranged on the desktop.

 The chapters in this book that cover procedures used in this project are Chapters 1, 2, and 9.

Chapter 21

Get ready to . . .

Create Desktop Shortcuts

1. Choose Start➪All Programs➪Accessories.

2. Right-click the Calculator item and choose Send
   To➪Desktop (Create Shortcut) (see Figure 21-1).

3. The shortcut appears on the desktop (see Figure 21-2).
   Right-click the desktop and choose Properties. Click
   the Desktop tab, and then click the Customize Desktop
   button.

4. In the resulting Desktop Items dialog box, select the My
   Documents check box to automatically display a shortcut for the My Documents folder.

5. Click OK twice to save the settings.

 Occasionally Windows offers to delete desktop icons that you haven't
used in a long time. Let it. The desktop should be reserved for frequently used programs, files, and folders. You can always re-create
shortcuts easily if you begin to use them again. To clean up your
desktop, manually right-click the desktop and choose Properties. On
the Desktop tab, click the Customize Desktop button. In the Desktop
Items dialog box that appears, click the Clean Desktop Now button,
which runs the Clean Desktop Wizard, which offers you options for
removing little-used shortcuts.

 If you're working on a project, consider creating a shortcut to that
project folder. Or, if you're figuring out your way around Windows,
consider creating a shortcut to the Help and Support Center.

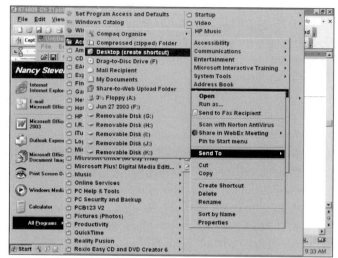

Figure 21-1: The Send To shortcut menu

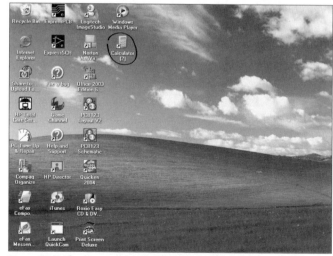

Figure 21-2: The shortcut to the Calculator placed on the desktop

Add an Application Shortcut to the Quick Launch Bar

1. On the taskbar, locate the Quick Launch bar just to the right of the Start button (see Figure 21-3).

    The Quick Launch bar is a feature of the taskbar. If it doesn't appear, from the Windows desktop, right-click the taskbar and choose Toolbars ➪Quick Launch.

2. Click the icon on the Windows desktop representing your antivirus software (if you don't have antivirus software, you should get some today!) and drag it to the Quick Launch bar (see Figure 21-4).

3. To launch your antivirus software, click its icon on the Quick Launch bar, or if you haven't used it recently you might need to click the arrow at the right of the Quick Launch bar and then click the software name on the pop-up list that appears.

    If you don't have antivirus software, you can do these steps with the icon of any program that you have on your desktop. The benefit of the Quick Launch bar is that it contains the programs that you use most often so that you don't have to locate those icons on a crowded desktop.

    After you place a shortcut on the Quick Launch bar, consider deleting it from the desktop. That can make your desktop easier to navigate. Don't worry: Deleting a shortcut doesn't delete an application, file, or folder.

Figure 21-3: The Quick Launch bar

Figure 21-4: The Quick Launch icon for Norton AntiVirus launches the application

Arrange Icons on the Desktop

1. Right-click the Windows desktop and in the resulting shortcut menu, shown in Figure 21-5, choose Arrange Icons By, and then choose Type.

2. Make sure that Auto Arrange isn't selected. (If it is selected, deselect it.) Now you can click any icon and drag it to another location on the desktop.

3. Click the Recycle Bin icon on the desktop and drag it to a new location separate from other desktop icons so you can find it easily (see Figure 21-6).

 If you've rearranged your desktop by moving items hither and yon, and you just long to snap icons into orderly rows along the left side of your desktop, consider the Auto Arrange feature. Right-click the desktop, choose Arrange By⇨Auto Arrange.

 Want to quickly hide all your desktop icons? Say the boss is headed your way and all you've got there is games? Right-click the desktop and choose Arrange Icons By⇨Show Desktop Icons. Poof! They're all gone. Just repeat the process and they're back again.

Figure 21-5: The desktop shortcut menu

Figure 21-6: The Recycle Bin icon moved across the desktop

Project: Create an Invitation

Do you long for the artist's life? Do you spend your Saturday nights pasting photos into scrapbooks and hand-making your own party invitations?

You're in luck: In this project, you get to be creative. First, you have to find a picture that you think is really neat (yourself on vacation, your kid in a school play, or your dog having a very much needed bath, for instance). Next you scan the photo, manipulate it to add text and colors, and insert it into a simple invitation that you design in WordPad.

You can do amazing things with Window's own built in applications. But if you have more high-powered software, feel free to replace WordPad or Paint in this project with a more sophisticated word processing or desktop publishing package to help you add more impact.

Chapter 3 covers built-in applications such as the scanner feature, Paint, and WordPad, which are used in this chapter. If you also want to add text formatting effects or insert other objects, check out Chapter 20.

Scan a Family Photo

1. Place your favorite family photo in your scanner.

2. Choose Start➪All Programs➪Accessories➪Scanner and Camera Wizard.

3. In the resulting Scanner and Camera Wizard, choose your preferences for scanning by selecting the Color Picture radio button.

4. Click Next. The Picture Name and Destination window appears, as shown in Figure 22-1.

5. In the first drop-down list, enter a name for a group of pictures or select a group that you've already created.

6. In the second drop-down list, select a format for the file, such as .bmp or .jpg.

7. In the third drop-down list, enter a location to store the file (for example, the My Pictures folder of My Documents is a good choice). Click Next.

8. In the resulting window, you see that the image is being scanned. Feel free to read the Sunday comics while your scanner and computer do what they were built for.

9. When the scanning is complete, you have three options (see Figure 22-2); select the third option, the one that starts with Nothing. Your image is now saved and ready for you to use.

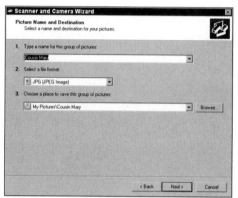

Figure 22-1: The Scanner and Camera Wizard, Picture Name and Destination window

 You aren't limited to scanning a photo; you can scan a document, a piece of fabric to use as a background image, a sketch, or just about anything that you can fit into your scanner. Experiment and have fun!

 When you save an image in a particular format, consider what software program you want to use to edit or work with the image and what formats that program supports. For example, Paint allows you to save in .bmp, .jpeg, .gif, .tiff, and .png image formats.

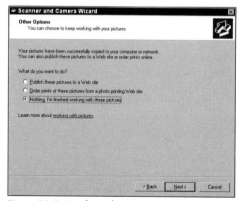

Figure 22-2: Completing the scan

Edit the Photo in Paint

1. Choose Start⇨All Programs⇨Accessories⇨Paint.

2. In the resulting Paint window (see Figure 22-3), choose File⇨Open. Locate the picture file that you scanned in the previous task, select it, and click Open.

3. Now click a color on the color palette in the bottom-left corner and then click the Airbrush tool (which shows a small spray can). Click and drag around the edge of the picture to apply a colorful border to the image.

4. Select the Text tool (the one with the capital A) and then click and drag the top-right corner of the image (or wherever seems to be a good spot on your particular photo) to create a text box. Enter appropriate invitation text.

5. Choose View⇨Text Toolbar, and use the tools there to change the font style to Bradley Hand ITC, 18 point, Bold (see Figure 22-4) or another decorative font on your computer.

6. Choose File⇨Save As, enter the filename **My Invitation**, choose a location to save your masterpiece, and then click OK.

 Paint has lots of great tools for drawing on images, adding colors, and modifying images by stretching or skewing them or flipping them around. Feel free to experiment!

 If you want to get rid of a part of your photo, try the Eraser tool (it looks like a little chalkboard eraser) or click the Select tool, click and drag an area of the image, and then right-click and choose Cut from the shortcut menu.

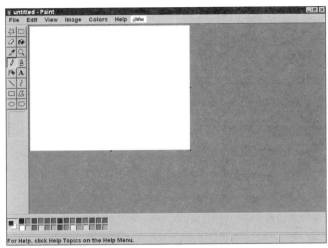

Figure 22-3: The Paint window

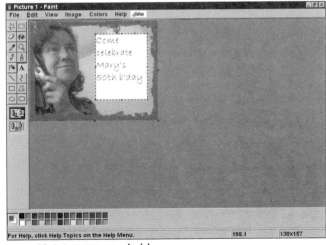

Figure 22-4: An invitation to a birthday party

Create an Invitation in WordPad

1. Choose Start⇨All Programs⇨Accessories⇨WordPad to open the WordPad window.

2. Enter lines of text, modifying to your own event as you please. (*Note:* Press Enter to create blank lines between text.)

3. Click and drag to select the text, and then choose Format⇨Font.

4. In the resulting Font dialog box, shown in Figure 22-5, change the Font setting to Copperplate Gothic Light, change the Size setting to 36 points, and apply the Bold effect.

5. Change the font color to a bright green and click OK to apply the settings.

6. Open your photo in Paint and choose Edit⇨Select All, and then right-click the image, and choose Copy.

7. In the WordPad file, click in the document on the line below the text and click the Paste button on the toolbar (see Figure 22-6).

8. Modify the inserted object however you want (moving it, resizing it, and so on).

9. When your document is complete, choose File⇨Save. In the Save As dialog box, enter a name in the File Name text box, select a file location from the Save In drop-down list, and then click Save.

 When an image is inserted into a document, it is sometimes way too big. To resize an image, click it to select it, and then place the mouse over a corner until a line with two arrows appears. Click and drag inward to make the image smaller, and drag outward to make it bigger.

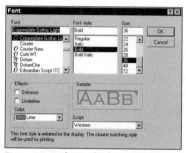

Figure 22-5: The WordPad Font dialog box

 In more sophisticated programs, such as Word or Publisher, you can modify the way text wraps around images so that it fits around the edges, or even runs right over the image. WordPad has no such feature. If you enter another line of text, you simply move the image down another line.

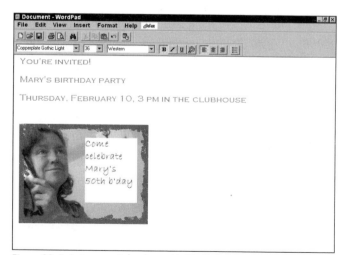

Figure 22-6: An image copied and pasted in WordPad

Project: Research Your Past

Everybody's into genealogy these days. Why should you be any different? Don't you long to find out if your great-great-great grandfather was a prince, an artist, or a diplomat? Even if you find out he was a horse thief, you might have a fun fact that you can use to shake up the next family reunion!

In this project, you get to explore some genealogy-related sites and find out a bit about your family history. You use the Internet Explorer (IE) browser to navigate your way around the Web, and you use its search feature to locate your ancestors. You also save a Web site to the Favorites folder so that you can quickly return there. To wrap the project up, you download a file to your computer.

 Chapter 5 on browsing the Web with IE covers the procedures used in this project.

Get ready to . . .

Search the Internet

1. Double-click the Internet Explorer icon on your desktop to open IE.

2. Click the Search button on the Standard toolbar.

3. In the resulting Search pane, click the Search the Internet link.

4. Enter search terms in the text box labeled Type Your Question Below (see Figure 23-1). Click Search.

5. In the resulting list of links, click a link to go that Web page or to provide additional search information.

6. Click the Back button in the Search pane to return to the previous page.

7. Enter **www.google.com** in your Address bar and click Go, and then enter a new search term, **Genealogy** and click the Google Search button.

8. In the listing (see Figure 23-2) that appears, click the Genealogy.com link (or another genealogy site if Genealogy.com doesn't appear in your results).

 When searching for your family name, consider adding another keyword, such as Wisconsin if much of your family is from there, or add a particular date if you're looking for an ancestor who lived during an earlier time period. This narrows down the results somewhat to help you find what you need.

 Try using other search engines to get slightly different results. A few popular ones are www.northernlight.com, www.yahoo.com, www.dogpile.com, and www.ask.com.

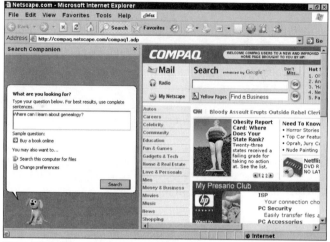

Figure 23-1: Enter a Search term or query

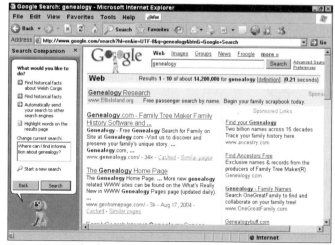

Figure 23-2: Results of a Google search

Add a Web Site to Your Favorites

1. With the Web site you visited in the previous task displayed, choose Favorites⇨Add to Favorites.

2. In the resulting Add Favorite dialog box, shown in Figure 23-3, modify the name of the Favorite listing to Genealogy Site. Click OK to add the site.

3. You can now go to your Favorite site in a couple different ways:

   - Choose the Favorites menu and then choose the name of the site from the list that's displayed.

   - Click the Favorites button on the Standard toolbar, and your favorites are displayed in the Favorites pane (see Figure 23-4). Click the site name to go there.

You can organize Favorites by clicking the Organize button at the top of the Favorites pane. Here you can create folders to break up Favorites into categories, rename, or delete favorite sites.

Another quick way to add a Web site to Favorites is to simply right-click the page and choose Add to Favorites from the shortcut menu that appears.

Figure 23-3: The Add Favorite dialog box

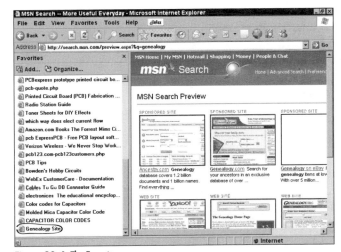

Figure 23-4: The Favorites pane

Download a File

1. Enter **www.census.gov** into your Address Bar and click Go.

2. On the Census Bureau Web site that appears (see Figure 23-5), click the Access Tools link.

3. On the resulting page, scroll down to the Downloadable Software section.

4. Click a link, such as CSPro, to begin the download process.

5. On the page that appears, click the Download link.

6. In the Download Information form that appears (see Figure 23-6), enter your information and deselect the Check This Box check box at the bottom so that you don't get mailings from the site (unless you really want to!).

7. Click the Submit Form button.

8. On the page that appears, click the To Continue the Download Click Here link.

9. On the Download CSPro page, click the Download CSPro link. In the resulting dialog box, click Save.

 CSPro can be useful if you get seriously into genealogy and want to compile census data. However, these steps are just an example of a product that you can download for free. If you find something else that you'd rather download, go for it.

 Always be cautious when downloading files from the Internet. First, download only from reputable sources. Second, be sure that you have an antivirus program installed that scans files as they're downloading or that you can use to scan all files on your hard drive periodically to keep viruses at bay.

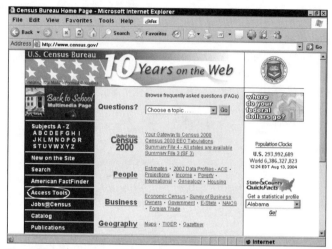

Figure 23-5: The U.S. Census Bureau site

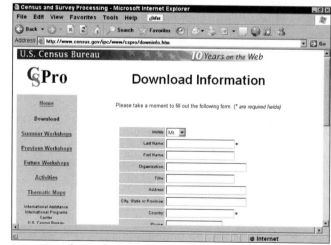

Figure 23-6: The Download Information form

Project: Creating an E-Mail Announcement

*R*emember the last time you changed your address, got a promotion, or had a baby? (Well, yeah, hopefully you at least remember having a baby.) You might have sent out an e-mail, addressing it to each and every person in your day planner address list with a quick (and pretty standard) note to let them know the good news.

In this project, I show you how to:

➡ Save yourself a lot of work by creating an e-mail group of all your friends in Outlook Express so that you can address that next message in just one step instead of entering addresses one at a time.

➡ Play around with using Outlook Express stationary and font formatting to make your announcement much more exciting.

➡ Add an attachment (a picture of the baby, a picture of your new house, or whatever) to make your e-mail announcement much more personal.

Chapter 6 on sending and receiving e-mail with Outlook Express covers the procedures used in this project.

Create an E-Mail Address Group in Outlook Express

1. In the Outlook Express main window, click the Addresses button to open the Address Book window.

2. To create a new group in the resulting Address Book window, click the New button and choose New Group from the menu that appears.

3. In the resulting Properties dialog box, enter a name in the Group Name text box (such as Friends, Soccer Car Pool, or Neighbors; see Figure 24-1).

4. Click the Select Members button.

5. In the Select Group Members dialog box, shown in Figure 24-2, click a contact in the list of names, and then click the Select button. Repeat this procedure for all the names that you want to be in the group, and then click OK.

6. To create a new contact (a contact that doesn't yet exist in your Address Book but that you would like to add to this group and add to the Address book), click the New Contact button.

7. In the resulting Properties dialog box, enter the contact information, and then click OK.

8. To add a person to the group but *not* to your Address Book, enter information in the Name and E-Mail text boxes, and click the Add button.

9. Click OK to save the group.

 After you create a group, just address a message to that group as you would to any other contact. Selecting the single group address inserts all the e-mail addresses in one step.

Figure 24-1: The Address Book Properties dialog box

 If a group is an organization with an address (for example, you create a group including several people in your office who share a mailing address and main phone number), use the Group Details tab to enter the group's address, phone, and so on.

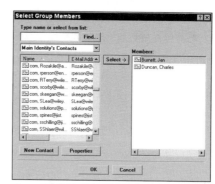

Figure 24-2: The Select Group Members dialog box

Create an E-Mail Message with Stationery

1. Click the arrow on the Create Mail button in the Outlook Express main window and choose the Select Stationery command to get more choices.

2. In the Select Stationery dialog box that appears (see Figure 24-3), select a stationery design from the list displayed, and then click OK.

3. Enter announcement text in the message section of the e-mail form that appears.

4. Select the text so that you can format it.

5. Use some of the following options to make changes to the font (see Figure 24-4 to get ideas from a formatted message):

   • **Font drop-down list:** Select a font from the drop-down list to apply it to the text.

   • **Font Size drop-down list:** Change the font size.

   • **Paragraph Style button:** Apply a preset style, such as Heading 1 or Address.

   • **Bold, Italic, and Underline buttons:** Apply styles to selected text.

   • **Font Color button:** Click to reveal a preset color palette to format fonts.

   • **Align Left, Center, Align Right, or Justify buttons:** Adjust the alignment.

 You can also create your own stationary. In the Select Stationery dialog box, click the Create New button to start the Stationery Setup Wizard. This allows you to select from a set of graphic templates, modify locations on the page of the graphic images or borders, and add background colors.

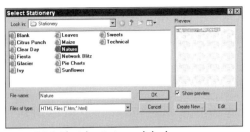

Figure 24-3: The Select Stationery dialog box

 Avoid using too many fonts and font effects in e-mail. This can make your e-mails difficult to read on-screen or when printed out. Also, consider using people-friendly fonts, such as Verdana, which was actually designed to be easily read on a computer screen.

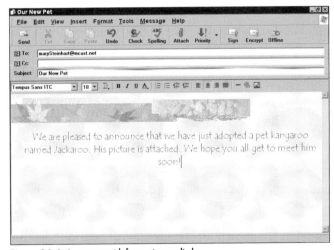

Figure 24-4: A message with formatting applied

Attach a Document and Send an E-Mail

1. Click the To button and select the group that you created in the first task of this chapter.

2. Click the Attach button.

3. In the Insert Attachment dialog box that appears (see Figure 24-5), locate a document that you want to attach by using the Look In drop-down list and the File Name text box, and then click Attach. (If you've done the tasks in Chapter 22, you could try using the image you scanned in that chapter.)

4. With the name of the attached file now in the Attach text box (see Figure 24-6), click the Send button to send the message to your entire group.

 Avoid sending overly large attachments. Some e-mail servers can't handle big files. Because of this, you might not be able to send the message before your own server times out, and even if you can send it, some recipients might not be able to receive it.

 Consider whether all the recipients can open your attachments. They would either have to have the program the attachment was created in, such as Excel or Quicken, or have a viewer. For example, a PowerPoint presentation can actually be packaged with a viewer so the recipient doesn't have to have PowerPoint to view the presentation. Another option is to save attachments as Adobe Acrobat documents. Anybody with Acrobat Reader (which is available online for free download at www.adobe.com) can view these documents.

Figure 24-5: The Insert Attachment dialog box

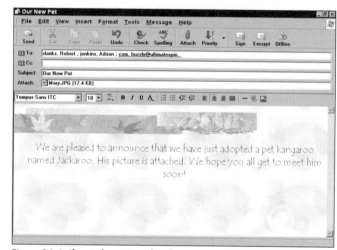

Figure 24-6: The attachment is ready to be sent

Project: Spiffing Up Your Desktop

I don't know about you, but I practically live at my computer for hours at a time. Being a writer, it's pretty much part of my job description to sit and stare at the screen for hours in procrastination mode, waiting for that next great idea to come. After a few hours of looking at that rolling green field and blue skies of the Windows desktop theme, I'm desperate for a change of view.

If you often have moments of wishing that you could look at anything but that field or that 3D flying screen saver thingie, this project will make you very happy. In this project, you make changes to the way your desktop looks. You play around with choosing a new theme, creating a custom color scheme, choosing a screen saver, and making settings for how the screen saver behaves.

By the time you're done, you'll have a much more exciting working environment.

 Chapter 9 on customizing the Windows desktop covers the procedures used in this project.

Change Your Desktop Background

1. Choose Start➪Control Panel and in Category View, click the Appearance and Themes link.

2. In the Appearance and Themes window that appears, click the Change the Desktop Background link.

3. On the resulting Desktop tab (see Figure 25-1), select Moon Flower from the Background list box.

4. Select the Tile option from the Position drop-down list.

5. Click OK to apply the background (see Figure 25-2).

 If you have a photo or other image that you would like to use as a background, you can always click the Browse button on the Desktop tab and locate it to make it available in the Background list box.

 To display your online home page on your desktop, in the Desktop tab of the Appearance and Themes window, click the Customize Desktop button, and then click the Web tab. Click on your home page, click the Synchronize button, and then click OK.

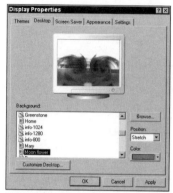

Figure 25-1: The Display Properties dialog box, Desktop tab

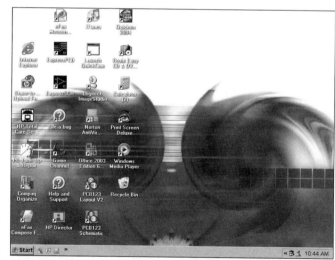

Figure 25-2: The Moon Flower background applied to the desktop

Apply a Custom Color Scheme

1. Right-click the desktop and choose Properties.

2. In the resulting Display Properties dialog box, click the Appearance tab, as shown in Figure 25-3.

3. Select a color scheme from the Color Scheme drop-down list.

4. To customize the selected preset color scheme, click the Advanced button.

5. In the resulting Advanced Appearance dialog box, shown in Figure 25-4, do the following to create a custom color scheme:

   • Select the Desktop option from the Item drop-down list. Then click the Color 1 button and select Red from the palette that appears.

   • Select the Active Title Bar option from the Item drop-down list. Then click the Color 1 button and select Teal.

   • Select the Inactive Title Bar option from the Item drop-down list. Then click the Color 1 button and select a bright green.

   • Select the Message Text option from the Item drop-down list. Then click the text Color 1 button and select a dark green color.

6. Click OK to close the Advanced Appearance dialog box, and then click the Themes tab on the Display Properties dialog box. On the Themes tab, click the Save As button, and then enter a theme name in the File Name text box and click Save.

7. Click OK to apply the new color scheme.

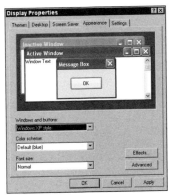

Figure 25-3: The Display Properties dialog box, Appearance tab

Figure 25-4: The Advanced Appearance dialog box

 Do you hate the new colors? To each his own! Just go to the Themes tab of the Display Properties dialog box and select another theme from the Theme drop-down list.

 Want to delete a theme? On the Themes tab of the Display Properties dialog box, select the theme in the Theme drop-down list, and then click the Delete button.

Change Your Screen Saver Settings

1. Right-click the desktop and choose Properties. Click the Screen Saver tab to display it, as shown in Figure 25-5.

2. In the Screen Saver drop-down list, select 3D Flower Box.

3. Click the Settings button. The 3D Flower Box Settings dialog box appears.

4. Click the Checkerboard radio button in the Coloring section and click OK.

5. Click the up or down spinner arrows on the Wait setting to adjust the wait time.

6. Click the Preview button, and you see the screen saver shown in Figure 25-6.

7. Click OK to close the Display Properties dialog box.

 Different screen savers have different settings available. Some allow you to control the speed or size of the graphic, and others, such as the BounceIt2, allow you to select different objects to be included. Experiment and play with the settings until everything rings your bell.

 The Wait setting controls how many minutes of inactivity occur before the screen saver displays. Inactivity means you don't press a key or move the mouse.

Figure 25-5: The Display Properties dialog box, Screen Saver tab

Figure 25-6: The 3D Flower Box screen saver

Project: Getting Help

Chapter

26

There's a reason most software companies now charge for technical support (besides greed): There's now so much help built into software like Windows XP, Microsoft has made it a virtually self-service environment.

You can search a huge database of information in the Windows Help and Support Center, tap into newsgroups online to get advice from other users, and use reference features such as a Windows Glossary to check techie and other terms. In this project, you use some of those features to find out about some Windows XP basics.

 Chapter 15 on getting help covers the procedures used in this project.

Get ready to . . .

Check Out What's New in Windows XP

1. Choose Start➪Help and Support.

2. In the Help and Support Center window, click the What's New in Windows XP link.

3. Click the Taking a Tour or Tutorial link.

4. Click the Take the Windows XP Tour link (see Figure 26-1).

5. At the opening window, click Next to proceed with the animated tour.

6. The tour appears (see Figure 26-2). Follow the directions provided by the narration.

   • To move to another part of the tour, click any icon at the bottom of the screen.

   • To stop the tour, click the Exit Tour button (the large red box with a white X).

 Did you get lost and want to start the tour again? Click the green icon with a circular arrow to restart the tour at any time.

 You might get sick of the background music. To turn the music off but leave the narration running, click the Music On/Off icon (a blue icon with musical notes on it). Click it again to turn the music back on.

 Many computer manufacturers customize the Help and Support Center to add their logo (such as Compaq or HP) and even a few extra help links specific to their own support programs. So don't get freaked out if your Help and Support Center looks slightly different than the ones shown here.

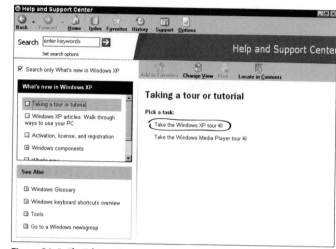

Figure 26-1: The Taking a Tour or Tutorial window

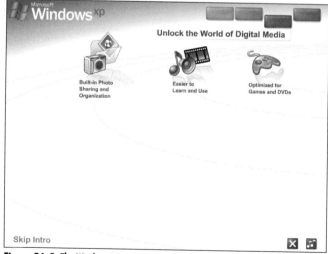

Figure 26-2: The Windows XP tour

Visit a Windows XP Newsgroup

1. From the main Help and Support Center window, click the Windows Basics link.

2. In the Windows Basics window, click the Go to a Windows Newsgroup link in the See Also section.

3. A Windows Newsgroup window appears; click the Go to Windows Newsgroups link.

4. In the Getting Started area of the Windows XP Newsgroups window (see Figure 26-3), click the Use Web-Based Reader link under the Windows XP General section.

5. In the resulting Discussions in Windows XP General window, click an item of interest to display it (see Figure 26-4). Try to click an item that has a post and at least one answer. (There is a plus sign to the left of the item; click it, and at least two items should appear beneath it: the posted question and at least one answer to it).

6. To close the Windows XP Newsgroups window, click the Close button in the upper-right corner.

 If you want to jump into the discussion with a posting displayed, click the Reply button. Enter your note in the Message area, select the I Accept radio button to accept the rules of use of the newsgroup, and then click the Post button. Note that you have to have a Windows Passport to participate in these discussions. If you don't have one, you can register on the resulting screen. If you do have one, you can enter your login ID and password to continue.

 If you want to filter the posts that you view, use the Show drop-down list to select the Answered Questions option or the Threads with Helpful Posts option. The first shows only questions that received responses; the second shows threads with answers that people considered helpful.

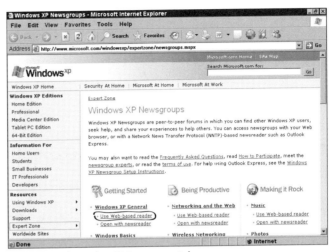

Figure 26-3: The Windows XP Newsgroups window

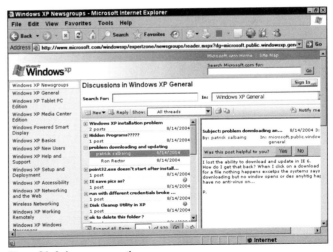

Figure 26-4: A newsgroup posting

Look Up a Term in Windows Glossary

1. Choose Start➪Help and Support.

2. In the Help and Support Center, click the Windows Basics link.

3. In the See Also pane of the window that appears, click the Windows Glossary link.

4. In the glossary that appears (see Figure 26-5), click the U letter icon.

5. Move your cursor over the thin bar along the left of the definitions pane. When your cursor forms two lines and arrows, click and drag to the left to enlarge the definitions pane (see Figure 26-6).

6. Scroll down in the list to locate the term Universal Resource Locator, and read the definition.

7. Click the Close button in the upper-right corner of the Help and Support Center window to close it.

 If you want to save a particular page of the glossary in your Help and Support Center favorites, just click the Add to Favorites button while viewing it.

 If you can't find a term in the glossary, consider entering it in the Search text box and clicking the Search icon (a red box with an arrow next to the Search text box).

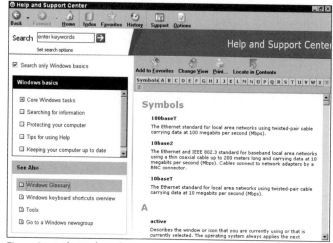

Figure 26-5: The Windows Glossary

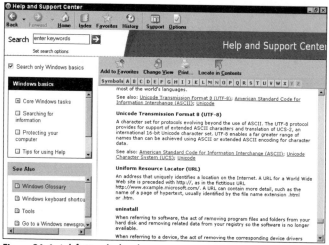

Figure 26-6: A definition displayed

Project: Get Musical

Music soothes the savage beast, and according to Thoreau, it is the universal language. So mastering the musical media features of your Windows XP computer can make you a citizen of the world with a passport to unlimited listening pleasure.

In this project, you create a playlist of jazz favorites, set yourself up to listen to a popular jazz station, and practice playing your favorite jazz CD.

Can you tell I like jazz? Don't worry: If country gets your toes tapping, or classical music sets you all aglow, feel free to make your own more appropriate choices as you go along in this project.

 Chapter 17 on playing music in Windows covers the procedures used in this project.

Create a Cool Playlist

1. Choose Start⟹All Programs⟹Accessories⟹Entertainment⟹ Windows Media Player.

2. In the resulting window, click the Media Library button, and then click the Playlists button and select the New Playlist option from the menu that appears.

3. In the resulting New Playlist dialog box (see Figure 27-1), enter **Jazz Favorites** in the Playlist Name text box.

4. Click the View Media Library by arrow and choose Genre from the drop down list. Double-click the Jazz Genre in the list to display all jazz songs.

5. Click on the "Highway Blues" title listed there and it's added to the playlist. Click OK.

6. Click the All Music option in the left pane of the Media Library, and its contents appear in the right pane (see Figure 27-2). Right-click another title listed in the right pane, and then choose Add to Playlist from the menu that appears.

7. In the Add to Playlist dialog box that appears, click the Jazz Favorites playlist and then click OK.

8. Repeat Step 4 to add another song to the Jazz Favorites playlist.

9. Under the My Playlists option in the left pane, click the Jazz Favorites playlist. Titles in the playlist appear in the list in the right pane (see Figure 27-2).

To play a title in a playlist, double-click it. Use the buttons at the bottom of the screen to stop, pause, or adjust the volume on the track being played.

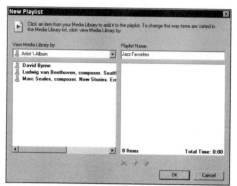

Figure 27-1: Naming a playlist

To get a cool video presentation for the song that's playing at the moment, click the Now Playing button. You even have controls for the colors and brightness of the video playback.

Figure 27-2: A playlist displayed in Media Library

Set Up a Radio Station

1. With Windows Media Player open, click the Radio Tuner button on the left.

2. In the resulting pane (see Figure 27-3), click the Jazz link in the Find More Stations area.

3. In the list of stations that appears (see Figure 27-4), click 101 FM, and then click the Add to My Stations link that appears.

4. Click the Visit Website to Play link; you might be prompted to download the Abacast streaming software. After it downloads, the station begins playing.

5. To stop the music, click the Stop button at the bottom of the Media Player window or click the Close button to close Windows Media Player.

After you save a station as a favorite, you can play it from the Radio Tuner pane by clicking the My Stations link shown in Figure 27-3 and clicking it on the list that's displayed.

If you don't find the station you want, you can search by keyword. In the Find More Stations area is a search text box. Enter a keyword such as **Swing** or station call letters such as **KQED** and Windows Media Player displays a list of matches.

Figure 27-3: The Radio Tuner main window

Figure 27-4: A list of available jazz stations

Play Music

1. Open Windows Media Player.

2. Click the Media Library button on the left to display the library shown in Figure 27-5. Click the Jazz Favorites playlist item in the left pane to open it; the titles of the songs appear in the right pane.

3. Double-click the "Highway Blues" item; it begins playing (see Figure 27-6).

4. Use the buttons at the bottom of the window to do the following:

   • Click the Stop button to stop playback.

   • Click the Next or Previous buttons to move to the next or previous track in the playlist.

   • Use the Mute and Volume controls to pump the sound up or down without having to modify the Windows volume settings.

 If you decide to move around Windows Media Player (for example going to the Radio Tuner to browse), the music continues playing until you stop it or start another track or radio station.

 Some radio stations might ask you to subscribe or provide your e-mail address. Be careful what you fill out if you don't want to get e-mails or be put on mailing lists.

Figure 27-5: The Media Library window

Figure 27-6: A tune playing in Media Player

Project: Movie Madness

This project is especially fun if you have your own camcorder and can upload a home movie to your computer. But for those of you who don't have your own images of little Suzy on the swings at the park or Fido munching your favorite slippers, you can use a sample movie provided with Windows XP.

To create a cinematic masterpiece in Windows XP, you use the Windows Movie Maker. First you create a project, and then you open a movie and organize clips in a storyboard. Then you can record your own narration (for which you need to have a microphone attached to your computer).

Let the moviemaking begin!

Chapter 18 on editing movies in Windows covers the procedures used in this project.

Create a Windows Movie Maker Project

1. Choose Start⊏➪All Programs⊏➪Accessories⊏➪Windows Movie Maker to open the Movie Maker window.

2. Choose File⊏➪New⊏➪Project to open a new blank Movie Maker file, and then save the file in the My Videos folder with the name My Movie Project.

3. Choose File⊏➪Import Into Collections to open the Import File dialog box.

4. The dialog box opens in the Movie Maker folder. Use the Look In drop-down list to locate the folder where the movie file that you want to open is saved. If you don't have a movie, use one of the sample files in the Movie Maker folder (see Figure 28-1).

5. Select the file, and then click the Import button to open the file in the Movie Maker window, as shown in Figure 28-2.

 You can also import a movie directly from your video camera. Simply click the Capture from Video Device link in the Movie Tasks pane of the Movie Maker, locate the device and follow the directions provided. If the Movie Tasks pane isn't visible, choose View⊏➪Task Pane.

 You can import one movie, place clips from it on the storyboard of your project, and then open other movies (one at a time) and add clips from them to your storyboard to create a movie edited together from various sources.

Figure 28-1: Locating a movie to import

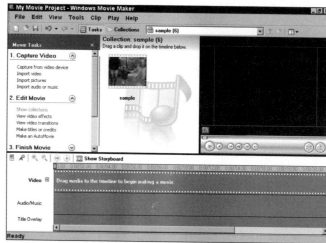

Figure 28-2: A movie opened in Movie Maker

Organize Clips in a Storyboard

1. With the My Movie Project file open in Movie Maker, if the Storyboard doesn't appear at the bottom of the screen, click the Show Timeline button. (*Note*: If the Storyboard is already displayed, that button will say Show Storyboard.)

2. In the Collection pane, click a movie clip and drag it to a box on the Storyboard, as shown in Figure 28-3. Repeat this with at least three other clips.

3. Click a clip and drag so that your mouse cursor rests on the line between the first and second adjacent clips. Release your mouse to insert the clip between the two others.

4. Click and drag the first clip and place it at the end (far right) of the Storyboard.

5. On the Storyboard, right-click the first clip and choose Copy. Then choose Edit⇨Paste to paste a copy next to the original. Click and drag the copy to the first blank space on the far right of the Storyboard. (Figure 28-4 shows clips arranged on the Storyboard.)

6. Click the Play button to play your movie from beginning to end.

7. When you finish editing your storyboard, be sure to save it by clicking the Save Project button (it looks like a little floppy disk) on the toolbar.

 Choosing Tools⇨Video Effects offers you a set of effects that you can add to your movie clips, such as adding transitions between clips (like fading into the next clip), making the film appear older (like an old black and white movie, for example), or adjusting the brightness settings.

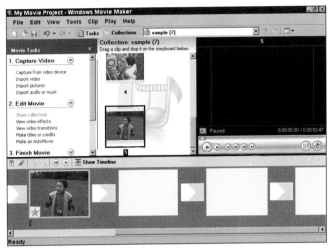

Figure 28-3: A clip placed on the Storyboard

Figure 28-4: A series of clips

Record a Narration

1. With your project open in Windows Movie Maker, click the Show Timeline button to display the Timeline view.

2. Choose Tools⇨Narrate Timeline.

3. In the resulting Narrate Timeline dialog box (see Figure 28-5), click the Input Level slider and drag it up or down to increase or decrease the record volume level.

4. Click the Start Narration button, and the video begins to play (see Figure 28-6). Begin speaking into your computer microphone. When you're done, click the Stop Narration button.

5. When the movie finishes running, a Save Windows Media File dialog box appears; click Save to save the narration (automatically named My Movie Project Narration) in the default Narration folder.

 You can record narrations only in the Timeline view, so if you have the Storyboard view displayed and try to record a narration, Movie Maker switches views and displays a dialog box informing you of the action.

 Narrations are saved as Windows Media Audio files with the .wma extension in the Narration folder within your My Videos folder. The file is opened and played automatically when you play your movie.

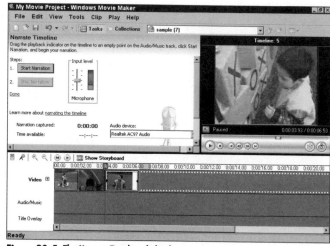

Figure 28-5: The Narrate Timeline dialog box

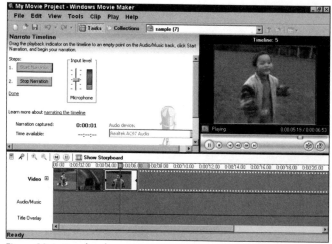

Figure 28-6: Recording the narration

Index

• T •